pytest Quick Start Guide

Write better Python code with simple and maintainable tests

Bruno Oliveira

BIRMINGHAM - MUMBAI

pytest Quick Start Guide

Commissioning Editor: Kunal Chaudhari
Acquisition Editor: Siddharth Mandal
Content Development Editor: Roshan Kumar
Technical Editor: Jinesh Topiwala
Copy Editor: Safis Editing
Project Coordinator: Hardik Bhinde
Proofreader: Safis Editing
Indexer: Priyanka Dhadke
Graphics: Jason Monteiro
Production Coordinator: Deepika Naik

First published: August 2018

Production reference: 2050918

Published by Packt Publishing Ltd.
Livery Place
35 Livery Street
Birmingham
B3 2PB, UK.

ISBN 978-1-78934-756-2

www.packtpub.com

`mapt.io`

Mapt is an online digital library that gives you full access to over 5,000 books and videos, as well as industry leading tools to help you plan your personal development and advance your career. For more information, please visit our website.

Why subscribe?

- Spend less time learning and more time coding with practical eBooks and Videos from over 4,000 industry professionals

- Improve your learning with Skill Plans built especially for you

- Get a free eBook or video every month

- Mapt is fully searchable

- Copy and paste, print, and bookmark content

PacktPub.com

Did you know that Packt offers eBook versions of every book published, with PDF and ePub files available? You can upgrade to the eBook version at `www.PacktPub.com` and, as a print book customer, you are entitled to a discount on the eBook copy. Get in touch with us at `service@packtpub.com` for more details.

At `www.PacktPub.com`, you can also read a collection of free technical articles, sign up for a range of free newsletters, and receive exclusive discounts and offers on Packt books and eBooks.

Foreword

pytest is one of the projects that show off the best qualities of Python; it is the easiest Python testing framework to get started and also the most powerful. The pytest developers leverage metaprogramming to help users; we can write tests as plain functions and use the assert keyword for checks, which means we can use any Python expression as a check, and we don't need to memorize the names of dozens of `assertThis`, `assertThat` methods. When there is a test failure, pytest uses sophisticated introspection to show the difference between the expected value and the value returned by the code under test. Introspection and decorators are also used to provide fixtures, parameters, grouping, skipping, and such like.

pytest is basically two parts: a library that gives you the API to write tests, and a test runner, a command-line utility that can search and execute tests across your project packages. The behavior of the pytest CLI can be configured in many ways, as described in this guide. By default, pytest is smart enough to collect tests written with the standard unittest package as well as doctest, running them and reporting all their results together. This means you can start using pytest now to run the tests you've already written with unittest and doctest.

pytest is very powerful out of the box, but it can also be enhanced by a large collection of industrial-strength plugins. A good collection of the best plugins is covered in this book.

If you are in the business of writing libraries and APIs for others to use, pytest is not only a great tool, but also a plentiful source of ideas and techniques, leveraging the best features of Python.

Anyone willing to learn pytest will be lucky to be guided by Bruno Oliveira, a long-time core developer of this most practical, powerful, and Pythonic package.

Thank you for your work on pytest, Bruno and for writing this book.

Valeu!

Luciano Ramalho
Principal consultant at Thoughtworks and author of Fluent Python

Contributors

About the author

Bruno Oliveira is a software developer with 18 years experience working at ESSS, developing desktop and web applications for simulation and numerical analysis for several industry sectors including oil and gas, aerospace, automotive, and chemical processes. Having taken part in the development of an internal testing framework to attend to the various needs of the applications he worked with, and having always been interested in testing and software quality, in 2012, Bruno took note of pytest and immediately fell in love with the project. He started contributing whenever he could and has been a pytest core contributor since 2014.

About the reviewers

Igor T. Ghisi is a software developer with a BSc in computer science and an MSc in computational mechanics. He has worked for 10 years in the largest research center in Latin America, in Rio de Janeiro, building software for R&D in engineering using agile practices, with a focus on the oil and gas industry. He developed software for 3D Mesh Generation, Mesh Visualization, Reservoir Simulation, Uncertainty, and Multi-disciplinary Optimization. He switched to web development over the last four years to solve engineering problems using web and cloud technologies.

Edson Tadeu Monteiro Manoel has more than 15 years' experience working in scientific software development, mostly using a mix of C++ and Python. He has been using pytest in his everyday work since 2013.

Packt is searching for authors like you

If you're interested in becoming an author for Packt, please visit `authors.packtpub.com` and apply today. We have worked with thousands of developers and tech professionals, just like you, to help them share their insight with the global tech community. You can make a general application, apply for a specific hot topic that we are recruiting an author for, or submit your own idea.

Table of Contents

Preface

Automated tests are a very important tool in a developer's tool belt. Having a set of automated tests not only increases productivity and software quality; it also works as a safety net for developers and gives confidence in relation to code refactorings. Python comes with a standard `unittest` module that is used to write automated tests, but there's an alternative: pytest. The pytest framework is simple to get started with, and scales from simple unit tests all the way through to complex integration testing. It is considered by many to be truly Pythonic in its approach, with simple functions, plain asserts, fixtures, plugins, and a whole plethora of features. More and more developers are adopting a full testing approach, so why not use a framework that is both simple and powerful and considered by many to be a true joy to use?

Who this book is for

This book is for anyone who wants to start using pytest to improve their testing skills in their daily workflow. It covers everything from getting pytest installed, and its more important features, all the way through to tips and tricks to converting existing `unittest`-based suites to pytest. There are also several tips and discussions based on the author's many years of testing and pytest experience. We go through several code examples in this book and only an intermediate level of Python is required, although you will enjoy the book even more if you have some `unittest` experience.

What this book covers

Chapter 1, *Introducing pytest*, discusses why testing is important, gives a quick overview of the standard `unittest` module, and finally takes a look at pytest's main features.

Chapter 2, *Writing and Running Tests*, covers pytest installation, how pytest uses only the `assert` statement for checking values, testing module organization, and some very useful command-line options for increased productivity.

Chapter 3, *Markers and Parametrization*, explains how pytest *markers* work, how to skip tests based on certain conditions, and discusses the difference between expected failures and flaky tests (and how to deal with them). Finally, we will learn how to use the `parametrize` mark to apply different sets of inputs to the same piece of testing code, avoiding repetition and inviting us to cover more input cases.

Chapter 4, *Fixtures*, explores one of pytest's more loved features, *fixtures*. We also go over some built-in fixtures, and finally some tips and tricks to get more out of fixtures in your test suite.

Chapter 5, *Plugins*, shows how to install and search for useful plugins in the rich plugin ecosystem, and it also goes over a series of assorted plugins that the author finds interesting and/or must have in their daily work.

Chapter 6, *Converting unittest suites to pytest*, visits a bunch of techniques that will help you start using pytest, even if all your tests are written in the unittest framework. It covers everything from running test suites out of the box with no changes, all the way to converting them to make use of pytest features with time-tested techniques.

Chapter 7, *Wrapping Up*, goes over the possible next steps if you want to consolidate your pytest skills. We also take a look at the friendly pytest community and how you can get more involved.

To get the most out of this book

Here's a short list of what you will need to get started:

- A desktop computer or laptop: pytest works in Linux, Windows, and macOS-X, so pick any system you prefer.
- Python 3: All examples are written in Python 3.6, but they should work with Python 3.4 or up with minor alternations, if any. Most examples can also be ported to Python 2 with a little more effort, but Python 3 is strongly recommended.
- Your favorite text editor or IDE to work on the code.
- Be comfortable with Python: nothing too advanced is required, but Python concepts, such as the with statement and decorators are important to have.

Download the example code files

You can download the example code files for this book from your account at www.packtpub.com. If you purchased this book elsewhere, you can visit www.packtpub.com/support and register to have the files emailed directly to you.

You can download the code files by following these steps:

1. Log in or register at `www.packtpub.com`.
2. Select the **SUPPORT** tab.
3. Click on **Code Downloads & Errata**.
4. Enter the name of the book in the **Search** box and follow the onscreen instructions.

Once the file is downloaded, please make sure that you unzip or extract the folder using the latest version of:

- WinRAR/7-Zip for Windows
- Zipeg/iZip/UnRarX for Mac
- 7-Zip/PeaZip for Linux

The code bundle for the book is also hosted on GitHub at `https://github.com/PacktPublishing/pytest-Quick-Start-Guide`. In case there's an update to the code, it will be updated on the existing GitHub repository.

We also have other code bundles from our rich catalog of books and videos available at `https://github.com/PacktPublishing/`. Check them out!

Conventions used

There are a number of text conventions used throughout this book.

`CodeInText`: Indicates code words in text, database table names, folder names, filenames, file extensions, pathnames, dummy URLs, user input, and Twitter handles. Here is an example: "Type this in your Command Prompt to create a `virtualenv`."

A block of code is set as follows:

```
# contents of test_player_mechanics.py
  def test_player_hit():
      player = create_player()
      assert player.health == 100
      undead = create_undead()
      undead.hit(player)
      assert player.health == 80
```

When we wish to draw your attention to a particular part of a code block, the relevant lines or items are set in bold:

```
def test_empty_name():
    with pytest.raises(InvalidCharacterNameError):
        create_character(name='', class_name='warrior')


def test_invalid_class_name():
    with pytest.raises(InvalidClassNameError):
        create_character(name='Solaire', class_name='mage')
```

Any command-line input or output is written as follows:

```
λ pip install pytest
```

Get in touch

Feedback from our readers is always welcome.

General feedback: Email feedback@packtpub.com and mention the book title in the subject of your message. If you have questions about any aspect of this book, please email us at questions@packtpub.com.

Errata: Although we have taken every care to ensure the accuracy of our content, mistakes do happen. If you have found a mistake in this book, we would be grateful if you would report this to us. Please visit www.packtpub.com/submit-errata, selecting your book, clicking on the Errata Submission Form link, and entering the details.

Piracy: If you come across any illegal copies of our works in any form on the internet, we would be grateful if you would provide us with the location address or website name. Please contact us at copyright@packtpub.com with a link to the material.

If you are interested in becoming an author: If there is a topic that you have expertise in and you are interested in either writing or contributing to a book, please visit authors.packtpub.com.

Reviews

Please leave a review. Once you have read and used this book, why not leave a review on the site that you purchased it from? Potential readers can then see and use your unbiased opinion to make purchase decisions, we at Packt can understand what you think about our products, and our authors can see your feedback on their book. Thank you!

For more information about Packt, please visit packtpub.com.

Introducing pytest 1

Automated testing is considered to be an indispensable tool and methodology for producing high-quality software. Testing should be a part of every professional software developer's toolbox, yet at the same time, it is considered by many to be a boring and repetitive part of the job. But that does not have to be the case when you use pytest as your testing framework.

This book will introduce you to various key features and will teach how to use pytest effectively in your day-to-day coding tasks right from the first chapter, focusing on making you productive as quickly as possible. Writing tests should then become a joy, rather than a boring part of the job.

We will start by taking a look at the reasons why automated testing is important. I will also try to convince you that it is not something that you should have simply because it is the right thing to do. Automated testing is something that you will want to have because it will make your job much **easier and more enjoyable**. We will take a glimpse at Python's standard `unittest` module, and introduce pytest and why it carries so much more punch while also being dead simple to get started with. Then, we will cover how to write tests, how to organize them into classes and directories, and how to use pytest's command line effectively. From there, we will take a look at how to use marks to control skipping tests or expecting test failures, how to use custom marks to your advantage, and how to test multiple inputs using the same testing code parameterization to avoid copy/pasting code. This will help us to learn how to manage and reuse testing resources and environments using one of pytest's most loved features: fixtures. After that, we will take a tour of some of the more popular and useful plugins from the vast plugin ecosystem that pytest has to offer. Finally, we will approach the somewhat more advanced topic of how to gradually convert `unittest` based test suites into the pytest style in order to take advantage of its many benefits in existing code bases.

In this chapter, we will take a quick look at why we should be testing, the built-in `unittest` module, and an overview of pytest. Here is what will be covered:

- Why spend time writing tests?
- A quick look at the `unittest` module
- Why pytest?

Let's get started by taking a step back and thinking about why writing tests is considered to be so important.

Why spend time writing tests?

Testing programs manually is natural; writing automated tests is not.

Programmers use various techniques when learning to code or when dabbling in new technologies and libraries. It is common to write short snippets, follow a tutorial, play in the REPL, or even use Jupyter (`http://jupyter.org/`). Often, this involves manually verifying the results of what is being studied by using print statements or plotting graphics. This is easy, natural, and a perfectly valid way of learning new things.

This pattern, however, should not be carried over to professional software development. Professional software is not simple; on the contrary, it is usually very complex. Depending on how well designed a system is, parts can be intertwined in strange ways, with the addition of new functionality potentially breaking another, apparently unrelated, part of the system. Fixing a bug might cause another bug to spring up somewhere else.

How can you make sure that a new functionality is working or that a bug has been squashed for good? Just as important, how can you ensure that, by fixing or introducing a new feature, another part of the system will not be broken?

The answer is by having a healthy and embracing suite of automated tests, also called a test suite.

A test suite is, simply put, code that tests your code. Usually, they create one or more necessary resources and call the application code under test. They then assert that the results are as expected. Besides being executed on the developer's machine, in most modern setups, they are run continuously—for example, every hour or every commit—by an automated system such as Jenkins. Because of this, adding tests for a piece of code means that, from now on, it will be tested again and again as features are added and bugs are fixed.

Having automated tests means that you can make changes to a program and immediately see if those changes have broken part of the system, acting as a safety net for developers. Having a good test suite is very liberating: you no longer fear improving a piece of code that was written 8 years ago, and if you make any mistakes, the test suite will tell you. You can add a new feature and be confident that it will not break any other parts of the system that you did not expect. It is absolutely essential to be able to convert a large library from Python 2 to 3 with confidence, or make large-scale refactorings. By adding one or more automated tests that reproduce a bug, and prove that you fixed it, you ensure the bug won't be reintroduced by refactoring or another coding error later down the road.

Once you get used to enjoying the benefits of having a test suite as a safety net, you might even decide to write tests for APIs that you depend on but know that developers don't have tests for: it is a rare moment of professional pride to be able to produce failing tests to the original developers to prove that their new release is to blame for a bug and not your code.

Having a well written and in-depth test suite will allow you to make changes, big or small, with confidence, and help you sleep better at night.

A quick look at the unittest module

Python comes with the built-in `unittest` module, which is a framework to write automated tests based on JUnit, a unit testing framework for Java. You create tests by subclassing from `unittest.TestCase` and defining methods that begin with `test`. Here's an example of a typical minimal test case using `unittest`:

```python
import unittest
from fibo import fibonacci

class Test(unittest.TestCase):

    def test_fibo(self):
        result = fibonacci(4)
        self.assertEqual(result, 3)

if __name__ == '__main__':
    unittest.main()
```

The focus of this example is on showcasing the test itself, not the code being tested, so we will be using a simple `fibonacci` function. The Fibonacci sequence is an infinite sequence of positive integers where the next number in the sequence is found by summing up the two previous numbers. Here are the first 11 numbers:

```
1, 1, 2, 3, 5, 8, 13, 21, 34, 55, 89, ...
```

Our `fibonacci` function receives an `index` of the fibonacci sequence, computes the value on the fly, and returns it.

To ensure the function is working as expected, we call it with a value that we know the correct answer for (the fourth element of the Fibonacci series is 3), then the `self.assertEqual(a, b)` method is called to check that `a` and `b` are equal. If the function has a bug and does not return the expected result, the framework will tell us when we execute it:

```
λ python3 -m venv .env
source .env/bin/activate
    F
    ================================================================
    FAIL: test_fibo (__main__.Test)
    ----------------------------------------------------------------
    Traceback (most recent call last):
      File "test_fibo.py", line 8, in test_fibo
        self.assertEqual(result, 3)
    AssertionError: 5 != 3


    ----------------------------------------------------------------
    Ran 1 test in 0.000s

    FAILED (failures=1)
```

It seems there's a bug in our `fibonacci` function and whoever wrote it forgot that for `n=0` it should return `0`. Fixing the function and running the test again shows that the function is now correct:

```
λ python test_fibo.py
    .
    ----------------------------------------------------------------
    Ran 1 test in 0.000s

    OK
```

This is great and is certainly a step in the right direction. But notice that, in order to code this very simple check, we had to do a number of things not really related to the check itself:

1. Import `unittest`
2. Create a class subclassing from `unittest.TestCase`

3. Use `self.assertEqual()` to do the checking; there are a lot of `self.assert*` methods that should be used for all situations like `self.assertGreaterEqual` (for ≥ comparisons), `self.assertLess` (for < comparisons), `self.assertAlmostEqual` (for floating point comparisons), `self.assertMultiLineEqual()` (for multi-line string comparisons), and so on

The above feels like unnecessary boilerplate, and while it is certainly not the end of the world, some people feel that the code is non-Pythonic; code is written just to placate the framework into doing what you need it to.

Also, the `unittest` framework doesn't provide much in terms of batteries included to help you write your tests for the real world. Need a temporary directory? You need to create it yourself and clean up afterwards. Need to connect to a PostgreSQL database to test a Flask application? You will need to write the supporting code to connect to the database, create the required tables, and clean up when the tests end. Need to share utility test functions and resources between tests? You will need to create base classes and reuse them through subclassing, which in large code bases might evolve into multiple inheritance. Some frameworks provide their own `unittest` support code (for example, Django, `https://www.djangoproject.com/`), but those frameworks are rare.

Why pytest?

Pytest is a mature and full-featured testing framework, from small tests to large scale functional tests for applications and libraries alike.

Pytest is simple to get started with. To write tests, you don't need classes; you can write simple functions that start with `test` and use Python's built-in `assert` statement:

```
from fibo import fibonacci

def test_fibo():
    assert fibonacci(4) == 3
```

That's it. You import your code, write a function, and use plain assert calls to ensure they are working as you expect: no need to make a subclass and use various `self.assert*` methods to do your testing. And the beautiful thing is that it also provides helpful output when an assertion fails:

```
λ pytest test_fibo2.py -q
F                                                                      [100%]
============================= FAILURES =============================
_____ test_fibo _____
```

```
    def test_fibo():
>       assert fibonacci(4) == 3
E       assert 5 == 3
E        + where 5 = fibonacci(4)

test_fibo2.py:4: AssertionError
1 failed in 0.03 seconds
```

Notice that the values involved in the expression and the code around it are displayed to make it easier to understand the error.

Pytest not only makes it **simple to write tests**, it has many **command-line options that increase productivity**, such as running just the last failing tests, or running a specific group of tests by name or because they're specially marked.

Creating and managing testing resources is an important aspect that is often overlooked in tutorials or overviews of testing frameworks. Tests for real-world applications usually need complex setups, such as starting a background worker, filling up a database, or initializing a GUI. Using pytest, those complex test resources can be managed by a powerful mechanism called **fixtures**. Fixtures are simple to use but very powerful at the same time, and many people refer to them as *pytest's killer feature*. They will be shown in detail in `Chapter 4`, *Fixtures*.

Customization is important, and pytest goes a step further by defining a very powerful **plugin** system. Plugins can change several aspects of the test run, from how tests are executed to providing new fixtures and capabilities to make it easy to test many types of applications and frameworks. There are plugins that execute tests in a random order each time to ensure tests are not changing global state that might affect other tests, plugins that repeat failing tests a number of times to weed out flaky behavior, plugins that show failures as they appear instead of only at the end of the run, and plugins that execute tests across many CPUs to speed up the suite. There are also plugins that are useful when testing Django, Flask, Twisted, and Qt applications, further plugins for the acceptance testing of web applications using Selenium. The number of external plugins is really staggering: at the time of writing, there are over 500 pytest plugins available to be installed and used right away (`http://plugincompat.herokuapp.com/`).

To summarize pytest:

- You use plain `assert` statements to write your checks, with detailed reporting
- pytest has automatic test discovery
- It has fixtures to manage test resources

- It has many, many plugins to expand its built-in capabilities and help test a huge number of frameworks and applications
- It runs `unittest` based test suites out of the box and without any modifications, so you can gradually migrate existing test suites

For these reasons, many consider pytest to be a Pythonic approach to writing tests in Python. It makes it easy to write simple tests and is powerful enough to write very complex functional tests. Perhaps more importantly, though, pytest makes testing fun.

Writing automated tests, and enjoying their many benefits, will become natural with pytest.

Summary

In this chapter, we covered why writing tests is important in order to produce high-quality software and to give you the confidence to introduce changes without fear. After that, we took a look at the built-in `unittest` module and how it can be used to write tests. Finally, we had a quick introduction to pytest, discovered how simple it is to write tests with it, looked at its key features, and also looked at the vast quantity of third-party plugins that cover a wide range of use cases and frameworks.

In the next chapter, we will learn how to install pytest, how to write simple tests, how to better organize them into files and directories within your project, and how to use the command line effectively.

Writing and Running Tests 2

In the previous chapter, we discussed why testing is so important and looked at a brief overview of the `unittest` module. We also took a cursory look at pytest's features, but barely got a taste of them.

In this chapter, we will start our journey with pytest. We will be pragmatic, so this means that we will not take an exhaustive look at all of the things it's possible to do with pytest, but instead provide you with a quick overview of the basics to make you productive quickly. We will take a look at how to write tests, how to organize them into files and directories, and how to use pytest's command line effectively.

Here's what is covered in this chapter:

- Installing pytest
- Writing and running tests
- Organizing files and packages
- Useful command-line options
- Configuration: `pytest.ini` file

 In the chapter, there are a lot of examples typed into the command line. They are marked by the λ character. To avoid clutter and to focus on the important parts, the pytest header (which normally displays the pytest version, the Python version, installed plugins, and so on) will be suppressed.

Let's jump right into how to install pytest.

Installing pytest

Installing pytest is really simple, but first, let's take a moment to review good practices for Python development.

All of the examples are for Python 3. They should be easy to adapt to Python 2 if necessary.

pip and virtualenv

The recommended practice for installing dependencies is to create a `virtualenv`. A `virtualenv` (https://packaging.python.org/guides/installing-using-pip-and-virtualenv/) acts like a complete separate Python installation from the one that comes with your operating system, making it safe to install the packages required by your application without risk of breaking your system Python or tools.

Now we will learn how to create a virtual environment and install pytest using pip. If you are already familiar with `virtualenv` and pip, you can skip this section:

1. Type this in your Command Prompt to create a `virtualenv`:

   λ **python -m venv .env**

2. This command will create a `.env` folder in the current directory, containing a full-blown Python installation. Before proceeding, you should `activate` the `virtualenv`:

   λ **source .env/bin/activate**

   Or on Windows:

   λ **.env\Scripts\activate**

   This will put the `virtualenv` Python in front of the `$PATH` environment variable, so Python, pip, and other tools will be executed from the `virtualenv`, not from your system.

3. Finally, to install pytest, type:

   λ **pip install pytest**

You can verify that everything went well by typing:

```
λ pytest --version
This is pytest version 3.5.1, imported from x:\fibo\.env36\lib\site-packages\pytest.py
```

Now, we are all set up and can begin!

Writing and running tests

Using pytest, all you need to do to start writing tests is to create a new file named
`test_*.py` and write test functions that start with `test`:

```
# contents of test_player_mechanics.py
def test_player_hit():
    player = create_player()
    assert player.health == 100
    undead = create_undead()
    undead.hit(player)
    assert player.health == 80
```

To execute this test, simply execute `pytest`, passing the name of the file:

```
λ pytest test_player_mechanics.py
```

If you don't pass anything, pytest will look for all of the test files from the current directory
recursively and execute them automatically.

 You might encounter examples on the internet that use `py.test` in the
command line instead of `pytest`. The reason for that is historical: pytest
used to be part of the `py` package, which provided several general
purpose utilities, including tools that followed the convention of starting
with `py.<TAB>` for tab completion, but since then, it has been moved into
its own project. The old `py.test` command is still available and is an alias
to `pytest`, but the latter is the recommended modern usage.

Note that there's no need to create classes; just simple functions and plain `assert`
statements are enough, but if you want to use classes to group tests you can do so:

```
class TestMechanics:

    def test_player_hit(self):
        ...

    def test_player_health_flask(self):
        ...
```

Grouping tests can be useful when you want to put a number of tests under the same scope: you can execute tests based on the class they are in, apply markers to all of the tests in a class (Chapter 3, *Markers and Parametrization*), and create fixtures bound to a class (Chapter 4, *Fixtures*).

Running tests

Pytest can run your tests in a number of ways. Let's quickly get into the basics now and, later on in the chapter, we will move on to more advanced options.

You can start by just simply executing the `pytest` command:

```
λ pytest
```

This will find all of the `test_*.py` and `*_test.py` modules in the current directory and below recursively, and will run all of the tests found in those files:

- You can reduce the search to specific directories:

```
λ pytest tests/core tests/contrib
```

- You can also mix any number of files and directories:

```
λ pytest tests/core tests/contrib/test_text_plugin.py
```

- You can execute specific tests by using the syntax `<test-file>::<test-function-name>`:

```
λ pytest tests/core/test_core.py::test_regex_matching
```

- You can execute all of the `test` methods of a `test` class:

```
λ pytest tests/contrib/test_text_plugin.py::TestPluginHooks
```

- You can execute a specific `test` method of a `test` class using the syntax `<test-file>::<test-class>::<test-method-name>`:

```
λ pytest tests/contrib/
test_text_plugin.py::TestPluginHooks::test_registration
```

The syntax used above is created internally by pytest, is unique to each test collected, and is called a `node id` or `item id`. It basically consists of the filename of the testing module, class, and functions joined together by the `::` characters.

Pytest will show a more verbose output, which includes node IDs, with the −v flag:

```
λ pytest tests/core -v
========================= test session starts =========================
. . .
collected 6 items

tests\core\test_core.py::test_regex_matching PASSED          [ 16%]
tests\core\test_core.py::test_check_options FAILED           [ 33%]
tests\core\test_core.py::test_type_checking FAILED           [ 50%]
tests\core\test_parser.py::test_parse_expr PASSED            [ 66%]
tests\core\test_parser.py::test_parse_num PASSED             [ 83%]
tests\core\test_parser.py::test_parse_add PASSED             [100%]
```

To see which tests there are without running them, use the `--collect-only` flag:

```
λ pytest tests/core --collect-only
========================= test session starts =========================
. . .
collected 6 items
<Module 'tests/core/test_core.py'>
  <Function 'test_regex_matching'>
  <Function 'test_check_options'>
  <Function 'test_type_checking'>
<Module 'tests/core/test_parser.py'>
  <Function 'test_parse_expr'>
  <Function 'test_parse_num'>
  <Function 'test_parse_add'>

==================== no tests ran in 0.01 seconds ====================
```

`--collect-only` is especially useful if you want to execute a specific test but can't remember its exact name.

Powerful asserts

As you've probably already noticed, pytest makes use of the built-in `assert` statement to check assumptions during testing. Contrary to other frameworks, you don't need to remember various `self.assert*` or `self.expect*` functions. While this may not seem like a big deal at first, after spending some time using plain asserts, you will realize how much that makes writing tests more enjoyable and natural.

Again, here's an example of a failure:

```
_____ test_default_health _____

    def test_default_health():
        health = get_default_health('warrior')
>       assert health == 95
E       assert 80 == 95

tests\test_assert_demo.py:25: AssertionError
```

Pytest shows the line of the failure, as well as the variables and expressions involved in the failure. By itself, this would be pretty cool already, but pytest goes a step further and provides specialized explanations of failures involving other data types.

Text differences

When showing the explanation for short strings, pytest uses a simple difference method:

```
_____ test_default_player_class _____

    def test_default_player_class():
        x = get_default_player_class()
>       assert x == 'sorcerer'
E       AssertionError: assert 'warrior' == 'sorcerer'
E         - warrior
E         + sorcerer
```

Longer strings show a smarter delta, using `difflib.ndiff` to quickly spot the differences:

```
_____ test_warrior_short_description _____

    def test_warrior_short_description():
        desc = get_short_class_description('warrior')
>       assert desc == 'A battle-hardened veteran, can equip heavy armor
and weapons.'
E       AssertionError: assert 'A battle-har... and weapons.' == 'A battle-
hard... and weapons.'
E         - A battle-hardened veteran, favors heavy armor and weapons.
E         ?                           ^ ^^^^
E         + A battle-hardened veteran, can equip heavy armor and weapons.
E         ?                           ^ ^^^^^^^
```

Multiline strings are also treated specially:

```
    def test_warrior_long_description():
        desc = get_long_class_description('warrior')
```

```
>         assert desc == textwrap.dedent('''\
              A seasoned veteran of many battles. Strength and Dexterity
              allow to yield heavy armor and weapons, as well as carry
              more equipment. Weak in magic.
              ''')
E         AssertionError: assert 'A seasoned v... \n' == 'A seasoned ve...
\n'
E           - A seasoned veteran of many battles. High Strength and Dexterity
E           ?                                        -----
E           + A seasoned veteran of many battles. Strength and Dexterity
E             allow to yield heavy armor and weapons, as well as carry
E           - more equipment while keeping a light roll. Weak in magic.
E           ?                  -----------------------------
E           + more equipment. Weak in magic.
```

Lists

Assertion failures for lists also show only differing items by default:

```
_____ test_get_starting_equiment _____

    def test_get_starting_equiment():
        expected = ['long sword', 'shield']
>       assert get_starting_equipment('warrior') == expected
E       AssertionError: assert ['long sword'...et', 'shield'] == ['long
sword', 'shield']
E         At index 1 diff: 'warrior set' != 'shield'
E         Left contains more items, first extra item: 'shield'
E         Use -v to get the full diff

tests\test_assert_demo.py:71: AssertionError
```

Note that pytest shows which index differs, and also that the -v flag can be used to show the complete difference between the lists:

```
_____ test_get_starting_equiment _____

    def test_get_starting_equiment():
        expected = ['long sword', 'shield']
>       assert get_starting_equipment('warrior') == expected
E       AssertionError: assert ['long sword'...et', 'shield'] == ['long
sword', 'shield']
E         At index 1 diff: 'warrior set' != 'shield'
E         Left contains more items, first extra item: 'shield'
E         Full diff:
E         - ['long sword', 'warrior set', 'shield']
E         ?                ---------------
```

```
E              + ['long sword', 'shield']
```

```
tests\test_assert_demo.py:71: AssertionError
```

If the difference is too big, pytest is smart enough to show only a portion to avoid showing too much output, displaying a message like the following:

```
E              ...Full output truncated (100 lines hidden), use '-vv' to show
```

Dictionaries and sets

Dictionaries are probably one of the most used data structures in Python, so, unsurprisingly, pytest has specialized representation for them:

```
_____ test_starting_health _____

    def test_starting_health():
        expected = {'warrior': 85, 'sorcerer': 50}
>       assert get_classes_starting_health() == expected
E       AssertionError: assert {'knight': 95...'warrior': 85} ==
{'sorcerer': 50, 'warrior': 85}
E           Omitting 1 identical items, use -vv to show
E           Differing items:
E           {'sorcerer': 55} != {'sorcerer': 50}
E           Left contains more items:
E           {'knight': 95}
E           Use -v to get the full diff
```

Sets also have similar output:

```
_____ test_player_classes _____

    def test_player_classes():
>       assert get_player_classes() == {'warrior', 'sorcerer'}
E       AssertionError: assert {'knight', 's...r', 'warrior'} ==
{'sorcerer', 'warrior'}
E           Extra items in the left set:
E           'knight'
E           Use -v to get the full diff
```

As with lists, there are also –v and –vv options for displaying more detailed output.

How does pytest do it?

By default, Python's assert statement does not provide any details when it fails, but as we just saw, pytest shows a lot of information about the variables and expressions involved in a failed assertion. So how does pytest do it?

Pytest is able to provide useful exceptions because it implements a mechanism called *assertion rewriting*.

Assertion rewriting works by installing a custom import hook that intercepts the standard Python import mechanism. When pytest detects that a test file (or plugin) is about to be imported, instead of loading the module, it first compiles the source code into an **abstract syntax tree** (**AST**) using the built-in `ast` module. Then, it searches for any `assert` statements and *rewrites* them so that the variables used in the expression are kept so that they can be used to show more helpful messages if the assertion fails. Finally, it saves the rewritten `pyc` file to disk for caching.

This all might seem very magical, but the process is actually simple, deterministic, and, best of all, completely transparent.

 If you want more details, refer to `http://pybites.blogspot.com.br/ 2011/07/behind-scenes-of-pytests-new-assertion.html`, written by the original developer of this feature, Benjamin Peterson. The `pytest-ast- back-to-python` plugin shows exactly what the AST of your test files looks like after the rewriting process. Refer to: `https://github.com/ tomviner/pytest-ast-back-to-python`.

Checking exceptions: pytest.raises

A good API documentation will clearly explain what the purpose of each function is, its parameters, and return values. Great API documentation also clearly explains which exceptions are raised and when.

For that reason, testing that exceptions are raised in the appropriate circumstances is just as important as testing the main functionality of APIs. It is also important to make sure that exceptions contain an appropriate and clear message to help users understand the issue.

Suppose we are writing an API for a game. This API allows programmers to write `mods`, which are a plugin of sorts that can change several aspects of a game, from new textures to complete new story lines and types of characters.

This API has a function that allows mod writers to create a new character, and it can raise exceptions in some situations:

```
def create_character(name: str, class_name: str) -> Character:
    """
    Creates a new character and inserts it into the database.

    :raise InvalidCharacterNameError:
        if the character name is empty.

    :raise InvalidClassNameError:
        if the class name is invalid.

    :return: the newly created Character.
    """
    ...
```

Pytest makes it easy to check that your code is raising the proper exceptions with the `raises` statement:

```
def test_empty_name():
    with pytest.raises(InvalidCharacterNameError):
        create_character(name='', class_name='warrior')


def test_invalid_class_name():
    with pytest.raises(InvalidClassNameError):
        create_character(name='Solaire', class_name='mage')
```

`pytest.raises` is a with-statement that ensures the exception class passed to it will be **raised** inside its execution **block**. For more details (https://docs.python.org/3/reference/compound_stmts.html#the-with-statement). Let's see how `create_character` implements those checks:

```
def create_character(name: str, class_name: str) -> Character:
    """
    Creates a new character and inserts it into the database.
    ...
    """
    if not name:
        raise InvalidCharacterNameError('character name empty')

    if class_name not in VALID_CLASSES:
        msg = f'invalid class name: "{class_name}"'
        raise InvalidCharacterNameError(msg)
    ...
```

If you are paying close attention, you probably noticed that the copy-paste error in the preceding code should actually raise an `InvalidClassNameError` for the class name check.

Executing this file:

```
======================= test session starts ========================
...
collected 2 items

tests\test_checks.py .F                                        [100%]

============================= FAILURES ==============================
_____ test_invalid_class_name _____

    def test_invalid_class_name():
        with pytest.raises(InvalidCharacterNameError):
>           create_character(name='Solaire', class_name='mage')

tests\test_checks.py:51:
_ _ _ _ _ _ _ _ _ _ _ _ _ _ _ _ _ _ _ _ _ _ _ _ _ _ _ _ _ _ _ _ _ _ _

name = 'Solaire', class_name = 'mage'

    def create_character(name: str, class_name: str) -> Character:
        """
        Creates a new character and inserts it into the database.

        :param name: the character name.

        :param class_name: the character class name.

        :raise InvalidCharacterNameError:
            if the character name is empty.

        :raise InvalidClassNameError:
            if the class name is invalid.

        :return: the newly created Character.
        """
        if not name:
            raise InvalidCharacterNameError('character name empty')

        if class_name not in VALID_CLASSES:
            msg = f'invalid class name: "{class_name}"'
>           raise InvalidClassNameError(msg)
E           test_checks.InvalidClassNameError: invalid class name: "mage"
```

```
tests\test_checks.py:40: InvalidClassNameError
================= 1 failed, 1 passed in 0.05 seconds =================
```

`test_empty_name` passed as expected. `test_invalid_class_name` raised `InvalidClassNameError`, so the exception was not captured by `pytest.raises`, which failed the test (as any other exception would).

Checking exception messages

As stated at the start of this section, APIs should provide clear messages in the exceptions they raise. In the previous examples, we only verified that the code was raising the appropriate exception type, but not the actual message.

`pytest.raises` can receive an optional `match` argument, which is a regular expression string that will be matched against the exception message, as well as checking the exception type. For more details, go to: `https://docs.python.org/3/howto/regex.html`. We can use that to improve our tests even further:

```python
def test_empty_name():
    with pytest.raises(InvalidCharacterNameError,
                       match='character name empty'):
        create_character(name='', class_name='warrior')


def test_invalid_class_name():
    with pytest.raises(InvalidClassNameError,
                       match='invalid class name: "mage"'):
        create_character(name='Solaire', class_name='mage')
```

Simple!

Checking warnings: pytest.warns

APIs also evolve. New and better alternatives to old functions are provided, arguments are removed, old ways of using a certain functionality evolve into better ways, and so on.

API writers have to strike a balance between keeping old code working to avoid breaking clients and providing better ways of doing things, while all the while keeping their own API code maintainable. For this reason, a solution often adopted is to start to issue `warnings` when API clients use the old behavior, in the hope that they update their code to the new constructs. Warning messages are shown in situations where the current usage is not wrong to warrant an exception, it just happens that there are new and better ways of doing it. Often, warning messages are shown during a grace period for this update to take place, and afterward the old way is no longer supported.

Python provides the standard warnings module exactly for this purpose, making it easy to warn developers about forthcoming changes in APIs. For more details, go to: `https://docs.python.org/3/library/warnings.html`. It lets you choose from a number of warning classes, for example:

- `UserWarning`: user warnings (`user` here means developers, not software users)
- `DeprecationWarning`: features that will be removed in the future
- `ResourcesWarning`: related to resource usage

(This list is not exhaustive. Consult the warnings documentation for the full listing. For more details, go to: `https://docs.python.org/3/library/warnings.html`).

Warning classes help users control which warnings should be shown and which ones should be suppressed.

For example, suppose an API for a computer game provides this handy function to obtain the starting hit points of player characters given their class name:

```
def get_initial_hit_points(player_class: str) -> int:
    ...
```

Time moves forward and the developers decide to use an `enum` instead of class names in the next release. For more details, go to: `https://docs.python.org/3/library/enum.html`, which is more adequate to represent a limited set of values:

```
class PlayerClass(Enum):
    WARRIOR = 1
    KNIGHT = 2
    SORCERER = 3
    CLERIC = 4
```

But changing this suddenly would break all clients, so they wisely decide to support both forms for the next release: `str` and the `PlayerClass` enum. They don't want to keep supporting this forever, so they start showing a warning whenever a class is passed as a `str`:

```
def get_initial_hit_points(player_class: Union[PlayerClass, str]) -> int:
    if isinstance(player_class, str):
        msg = 'Using player_class as str has been deprecated' \
            'and will be removed in the future'
        warnings.warn(DeprecationWarning(msg))
        player_class = get_player_enum_from_string(player_class)
    ...
```

In the same vein as `pytest.raises` from the previous section, the `pytest.warns` function lets you test whether your API code is producing the warnings you expect:

```
def test_get_initial_hit_points_warning():
    with pytest.warns(DeprecationWarning):
        get_initial_hit_points('warrior')
```

As with `pytest.raises`, `pytest.warns` can receive an optional `match` argument, which is a regular expression string. For more details, go to: `https://docs.python.org/3/howto/regex.html`, which will be matched against the exception message:

```
def test_get_initial_hit_points_warning():
    with pytest.warns(DeprecationWarning,
                      match='.*str has been deprecated.*'):
        get_initial_hit_points('warrior')
```

Comparing floating point numbers: pytest.approx

Comparing floating point numbers can be tricky. For more details, go to: `https://docs.python.org/3/tutorial/floatingpoint.html`. Numbers that we consider equal in the real world are not so when represented by computer hardware:

```
>>> 0.1 + 0.2 == 0.3
False
```

When writing tests, it is very common to compare the results produced by our code against what we expect as floating point values. As shown above, a simple == comparison often won't be sufficient. A common approach is to use a known tolerance instead and use `abs` to correctly deal with negative numbers:

```
def test_simple_math():
    assert abs(0.1 + 0.2) - 0.3 < 0.0001
```

But besides being ugly and hard to understand, it is sometimes difficult to come up with a tolerance that works in most situations. The chosen tolerance of `0.0001` might work for the numbers above, but not for very large numbers or very small ones. Depending on the computation performed, you would need to find a suitable tolerance for every set of input numbers, which is tedious and error-prone.

`pytest.approx` solves this problem by automatically choosing a tolerance appropriate for the values involved in the expression, providing a very nice syntax to boot:

```
def test_approx_simple():
    assert 0.1 + 0.2 == approx(0.3)
```

You can read the above as `assert that 0.1 + 0.2 equals approximately to 0.3`.

But the `approx` function does not stop there; it can be used to compare:

- Sequences of numbers:

```
def test_approx_list():
    assert [0.1 + 1.2, 0.2 + 0.8] == approx([1.3, 1.0])
```

- Dictionary `values` (not keys):

```
def test_approx_dict():
    values = {'v1': 0.1 + 1.2, 'v2': 0.2 + 0.8}
    assert values == approx(dict(v1=1.3, v2=1.0))
```

- `numpy` arrays:

```
def test_approx_numpy():
    import numpy as np
    values = np.array([0.1, 0.2]) + np.array([1.2, 0.8])
    assert values == approx(np.array([1.3, 1.0]))
```

When a test fails, `approx` provides a nice error message displaying the values that failed and the tolerance used:

```
    def test_approx_simple_fail():
>       assert 0.1 + 0.2 == approx(0.35)
E       assert (0.1 + 0.2) == 0.35 ± 3.5e-07
E        +  where 0.35 ± 3.5e-07 = approx(0.35)
```

Organizing files and packages

Pytest needs to import your code and test modules, and it is up to you how to organize them. Pytest supports two common test layouts, which we will discuss next.

Tests that accompany your code

You can place your test modules together with the code they are testing by creating a `tests` folder next to the modules themselves:

```
setup.py
mylib/
    tests/
          __init__.py
          test_core.py
          test_utils.py
    __init__.py
    core.py
    utils.py
```

By putting the tests near the code they test, you gain the following advantages:

- It is easier to add new tests and test modules in this hierarchy and keep them in sync
- Your tests are now part of your package, so they can be deployed and run in other environments

The main disadvantage with this approach is that some folks don't like the added package size of the extra modules, which are now packaged together with the rest of the code, but this is usually minimal and of little concern.

As an additional benefit, you can use the `--pyargs` option to specify tests using their module import path. For example:

```
λ pytest --pyargs mylib.tests
```

This will execute all test modules found under `mylib.tests`.

You might consider using `_tests` for the test module names instead of `_test`. This makes the directory easier to find because the leading underscore usually makes them appear at the top of the folder hierarchy. Of course, feel free to use `tests` or any other name that you prefer; pytest doesn't care as long as the test modules themselves are named `test_*.py` or `*_test.py`.

Tests separate from your code

An alternative to the method above is to organize your tests in a separate directory from the main package:

```
setup.py
mylib/
    __init__.py
    core.py
    utils.py
tests/
    __init__.py
    test_core.py
    test_utils.py
```

Some people prefer this layout because:

- It keeps library code and testing code separate
- The testing code is not included in the source package

One disadvantage of the above method is that, once you have a more complex hierarchy, you will probably want to keep the same hierarchy inside your tests directory, and that's a little harder to maintain and keep in sync:

```
mylib/
    __init__.py
    core/
        __init__.py
        foundation.py
    contrib/
        __init__.py
        text_plugin.py
tests/
    __init__.py
    core/
        __init__.py
        test_foundation.py
```

```
contrib/
    __init__.py
    test_text_plugin.py
```

 So, which layout is the best? Both layouts have advantages and disadvantages. Pytest itself works perfectly well with either of them, so feel free to choose a layout that you are more comfortable with.

Useful command-line options

Now we will take a look at command-line options that will make you more productive in your daily work. As stated at the beginning of the chapter, this is not a complete list of all of the command-line features; just the ones that you will use (and love) the most.

Keyword expressions: -k

Often, you don't exactly remember the full path or name of a test that you want to execute. At other times, many tests in your suite follow a similar pattern and you want to execute all of them because you just refactored a sensitive area of the code.

By using the `-k` `<EXPRESSION>` flag (from *keyword expression*), you can run tests whose `item id` loosely matches the given expression:

```
λ pytest -k "test_parse"
```

This will execute all tests that contain the string `parse` in their item IDs. You can also write simple Python expressions using Boolean operators:

```
λ pytest -k "parse and not num"
```

This will execute all tests that contain `parse` but not `num` in their item IDs.

Stop soon: -x, --maxfail

When doing large-scale refactorings, you might not know beforehand how or which tests are going to be affected. In those situations, you might try to guess which modules will be affected and start running tests for those. But, often, you end up breaking more tests than you initially estimated and quickly try to stop the test session by hitting CTRL+C when everything starts to fail unexpectedly.

In those situations, you might try using the `--maxfail=N` command-line flag, which stops the test session automatically after `N` failures or errors, or the shortcut `-x`, which equals `--maxfail=1`.

```
λ pytest tests/core -x
```

This allows you to quickly see the first failing test and deal with the failure. After fixing the reason for the failure, you can continue running with `-x` to deal with the next problem.

If you find this brilliant, you don't want to skip the next section!

Last failed, failed first: --lf, --ff

Pytest always remembers tests that failed in previous sessions, and can reuse that information to skip right to the tests that have failed previously. This is excellent news if you are incrementally fixing a test suite after a large refactoring, as mentioned in the previous section.

You can run the tests that failed before by passing the `--lf` flag (meaning last failed):

```
λ pytest --lf tests/core
...
collected 6 items / 4 deselected
run-last-failure: rerun previous 2 failures
```

When used together with `-x` (`--maxfail=1`) these two flags are refactoring heaven:

```
λ pytest -x --lf
```

This lets you start executing the full suite and then pytest stops at the first test that fails. You fix the code, and execute the same command line again. Pytest starts right at the failed test, and goes on if it passes (or stops again if you haven't yet managed to fix the code yet). It will then stop at the next failure. Rinse and repeat until all tests pass again.

Keep in mind that it doesn't matter if you execute another subset of tests in the middle of your refactoring; pytest always remembers which tests failed, regardless of the command-line executed.

If you have ever done a large refactoring and had to keep track of which tests were failing so that you didn't waste your time running the test suite over and over again, you will definitely appreciate this boost in your productivity.

Finally, the `--ff` flag is similar to `--lf`, but it will reorder your tests so the previous failures are run **first**, followed by the tests that passed or that were not run yet:

```
λ pytest -x --lf
========================= test session starts =========================
...
collected 6 items
run-last-failure: rerun previous 2 failures first
```

Output capturing: -s and --capture

Sometimes, developers leave `print` statements laying around by mistake, or even on purpose, to be used later for debugging. Some applications also may write to `stdout` or `stderr` as part of their normal operation or logging.

All that output would make understanding the test suite display much harder. For this reason, by default, pytest captures all output written to `stdout` and `stderr` automatically.

Consider this function to compute a hash of some text given to it that has some debugging code left on it:

```python
import hashlib

def commit_hash(contents):
    size = len(contents)
    print('content size', size)
    hash_contents = str(size) + '\0' + contents
    result = hashlib.sha1(hash_contents.encode('UTF-8')).hexdigest()
    print(result)
    return result[:8]
```

We have a very simple test for it:

```python
def test_commit_hash():
    contents = 'some text contents for commit'
    assert commit_hash(contents) == '0cf85793'
```

When executing this test, by default, you won't see the output of the `print` calls:

```
λ pytest tests\test_digest.py
========================= test session starts =========================
...

tests\test_digest.py .                                          [100%]

===================== 1 passed in 0.03 seconds =====================
```

That's nice and clean.

But those print statements are there to help you understand and debug the code, which is why pytest will show the captured output if the test **fails**.

Let's change the contents of the hashed text but not the hash itself. Now, pytest will show the captured output in a separate section after the error traceback:

```
λ pytest tests\test_digest.py
========================= test session starts =========================
. . .

tests\test_digest.py F                                            [100%]

============================== FAILURES ===============================
_____ test_commit_hash _____

    def test_commit_hash():
        contents = 'a new text emerges!'
>       assert commit_hash(contents) == '0cf85793'
E       AssertionError: assert '383aa486' == '0cf85793'
E         - 383aa486
E         + 0cf85793

tests\test_digest.py:15: AssertionError
------------------------ Captured stdout call -------------------------
content size 19
383aa48666ab84296a573d1f798fff3b0b176ae8
===================== 1 failed in 0.05 seconds ========================
```

Showing the captured output on failing tests is very handy when running tests locally, and even more so when running tests on CI.

Disabling capturing with -s

While running your tests locally, you might want to disable output capturing to see what messages are being printed in real-time, or whether the capturing is interfering with other capturing your code might be doing.

In those cases, just pass -s to pytest to completely disable capturing:

```
λ pytest tests\test_digest.py -s
========================= test session starts =========================
. . .

tests\test_digest.py content size 29
```

```
0cf857938e0b4a1b3fdd41d424ae97d0caeab166
.


===================== 1 passed in 0.02 seconds =====================
```

Capture methods with --capture

Pytest has two methods to capture output. Which method is used can be chosen with the `--capture` command-line flag:

- `--capture=fd`: captures output at the **file-descriptor level**, which means that all output written to the file descriptors, 1 (stdout) and 2 (stderr), is captured. This will capture output even from C extensions and is the default.
- `--capture=sys`: captures output written directly to `sys.stdout` and `sys.stderr` at the Python level, without trying to capture system-level file descriptors.

Usually, you don't need to change this, but in a few corner cases, depending on what your code is doing, changing the capture method might be useful.

For completeness, there's also `--capture=no`, which is the same as `-s`.

Traceback modes and locals: --tb, --showlocals

Pytest will show a complete traceback of a failing test, as expected from a testing framework. However, by default, it doesn't show the standard traceback that most Python programmers are used to; it shows a different traceback:

```
============================== FAILURES ==============================
_____ test_read_properties _____

 def test_read_properties():
  lines = DATA.strip().splitlines()
> grids = list(iter_grids_from_csv(lines))

tests\test_read_properties.py:32:
_ _ _ _ _ _ _ _ _ _ _ _ _ _ _ _ _ _ _ _ _ _ _ _ _ _ _ _ _ _ _ _ _ _
tests\test_read_properties.py:27: in iter_grids_from_csv
  yield parse_grid_data(fields)
tests\test_read_properties.py:21: in parse_grid_data
  active_cells=convert_size(fields[2]),
_ _ _ _ _ _ _ _ _ _ _ _ _ _ _ _ _ _ _ _ _ _ _ _ _ _ _ _ _ _ _ _ _ _
```

```
s = 'NULL'

 def convert_size(s):
> return int(s)
E ValueError: invalid literal for int() with base 10: 'NULL'

tests\test_read_properties.py:14: ValueError
====================== 1 failed in 0.05 seconds ======================
```

This traceback shows only a single line of code and file location for all frames in the traceback stack, except for the first and last one, where a portion of the code is shown as well (in bold).

While some might find it strange at first, once you get used to it you realize that it makes spotting the cause of the error much simpler. By looking at the surrounding code of the start and end of the traceback, you can usually understand the error better. I suggest that you try to get used to the default traceback provided by pytest for a few weeks; I'm sure you will love it and never look back.

If you don't like pytest's default traceback, however, there are other traceback modes, which are controlled by the --tb flag. The default is --tb=auto and was shown previously. Let's have a look at an overview of the other modes in the next sections.

--tb=long

This mode will show a **portion of the code for all frames** of failure tracebacks, making it quite verbose:

```
============================== FAILURES ==============================
_____ t_____

    def test_read_properties():
        lines = DATA.strip().splitlines()
>       grids = list(iter_grids_from_csv(lines))

tests\test_read_properties.py:32:
_ _ _ _ _ _ _ _ _ _ _ _ _ _ _ _ _ _ _ _ _ _ _ _ _ _ _ _ _ _ _ _

lines = ['Main Grid,48,44', '2nd Grid,24,21', '3rd Grid,24,null']

    def iter_grids_from_csv(lines):
        for fields in csv.reader(lines):
>           yield parse_grid_data(fields)

tests\test_read_properties.py:27:
```

```
- - - - - - - - - - - - - - - - - - - - - - - - - - - - - - - - - -
    fields = ['3rd Grid', '24', 'null']

        def parse_grid_data(fields):
            return GridData(
                name=str(fields[0]),
                total_cells=convert_size(fields[1]),
>               active_cells=convert_size(fields[2]),
                )

    tests\test_read_properties.py:21:
- - - - - - - - - - - - - - - - - - - - - - - - - - - - - - - - - -
    s = 'null'

        def convert_size(s):
>           return int(s)
E           ValueError: invalid literal for int() with base 10: 'null'

    tests\test_read_properties.py:14: ValueError
===================== 1 failed in 0.05 seconds =====================
```

--tb=short

This mode will show a single line of code from all the frames of the failure traceback, providing short and concise output:

```
============================= FAILURES =============================
_____ test_read_properties _____
tests\test_read_properties.py:32: in test_read_properties
    grids = list(iter_grids_from_csv(lines))
tests\test_read_properties.py:27: in iter_grids_from_csv
    yield parse_grid_data(fields)
tests\test_read_properties.py:21: in parse_grid_data
    active_cells=convert_size(fields[2]),
tests\test_read_properties.py:14: in convert_size
    return int(s)
E   ValueError: invalid literal for int() with base 10: 'null'
===================== 1 failed in 0.04 seconds =====================
```

--tb=native

This mode will output the exact same traceback normally used by Python to report exceptions and is loved by purists:

```
_____ test_read_properties _____
Traceback (most recent call last):
  File "X:\CH2\tests\test_read_properties.py", line 32, in
test_read_properties
    grids = list(iter_grids_from_csv(lines))
  File "X:\CH2\tests\test_read_properties.py", line 27, in
iter_grids_from_csv
    yield parse_grid_data(fields)
  File "X:\CH2\tests\test_read_properties.py", line 21, in parse_grid_data
    active_cells=convert_size(fields[2]),
  File "X:\CH2\tests\test_read_properties.py", line 14, in convert_size
    return int(s)
ValueError: invalid literal for int() with base 10: 'null'
===================== 1 failed in 0.03 seconds =====================
```

--tb=line

This mode will output a single line per failing test, showing only the exception message and the file location of the error:

```
============================= FAILURES =============================
X:\CH2\tests\test_read_properties.py:14: ValueError: invalid literal for
int() with base 10: 'null'
```

This mode might be useful if you are doing a massive refactoring and except a ton of failures anyway, planning to enter **refactoring-heaven mode** with the `--lf -x` flags afterwards.

--tb=no

This does not show any traceback or failure message at all, making it also useful to run the suite first to get a glimpse of how many failures there are, so that you can start using `--lf -x` flags to fix tests step-wise:

```
tests\test_read_properties.py F                              [100%]

===================== 1 failed in 0.04 seconds =====================
```

--showlocals (-l)

Finally, while this is not a traceback mode flag specifically, `--showlocals` (or `-l` as shortcut) augments the traceback modes by showing a list of the **local variables and their values** when using `--tb=auto`, `--tb=long`, and `--tb=short` modes.

For example, here's the output of `--tb=auto` and `--showlocals`:

```
_____ test_read_properties _____

    def test_read_properties():
        lines = DATA.strip().splitlines()
>       grids = list(iter_grids_from_csv(lines))

lines      = ['Main Grid,48,44', '2nd Grid,24,21', '3rd Grid,24,null']

tests\test_read_properties.py:32:
_ _ _ _ _ _ _ _ _ _ _ _ _ _ _ _ _ _ _ _ _ _ _ _ _ _ _ _ _ _ _ _ _ _
tests\test_read_properties.py:27: in iter_grids_from_csv
    yield parse_grid_data(fields)
tests\test_read_properties.py:21: in parse_grid_data
    active_cells=convert_size(fields[2]),
_ _ _ _ _ _ _ _ _ _ _ _ _ _ _ _ _ _ _ _ _ _ _ _ _ _ _ _ _ _ _ _ _ _

s = 'null'

    def convert_size(s):
>       return int(s)
E       ValueError: invalid literal for int() with base 10: 'null'

s          = 'null'

tests\test_read_properties.py:14: ValueError
====================== 1 failed in 0.05 seconds ======================
```

Notice how this makes it much easier to see where the bad data is coming from: the `'3rd Grid,24,null'` string that is being read from a file at the start of the test.

`--showlocals` is extremely useful both when running your tests locally and in CI, being a firm favorite. Be careful, though, as this might be a security risk: local variables might expose passwords and other sensitive information, so make sure to transfer tracebacks using secure connections and be careful to make them public.

Slow tests with --durations

At the start of a project, your test suite is usually blazingly fast, running in a few seconds, and life is good. But as projects grow in size, so do their test suites, both in the number of tests and the time it takes for them to run.

Having a slow test suite affects productivity, especially if you follow TDD and run tests all the time. For this reason, it is healthy to periodically take a look at your longest running tests and perhaps analyze whether they can be made faster: perhaps you are using a large dataset in a place where a much smaller (and faster) dataset would do, or you might be executing redundant steps that are not important for the actual test being done.

When that happens, you will love the `--durations=N` flag. This flag provides a summary of the N longest running tests, or uses zero to see a summary of all tests:

```
λ pytest --durations=5
. . .
===================== slowest 5 test durations =======================
3.40s call CH2/tests/test_slow.py::test_corner_case
2.00s call CH2/tests/test_slow.py::test_parse_large_file
0.00s call CH2/tests/core/test_core.py::test_type_checking
0.00s teardown CH2/tests/core/test_parser.py::test_parse_expr
0.00s call CH2/tests/test_digest.py::test_commit_hash
================= 3 failed, 7 passed in 5.51 seconds =================
```

This output provides invaluable information when you start hunting for tests to speed up.

Although this flag is not something that you will use daily, because it seems that many people don't know about it, it is worth mentioning.

Extra test summary: -ra

Pytest shows rich traceback information on failing tests. The extra information is great, but the actual footer is not very helpful in identifying which tests have actually failed:

```
. . .
_____ test_type_checking _____

    def test_type_checking():
>       assert 0
E       assert 0

tests\core\test_core.py:12: AssertionError
================ 14 failed, 17 passed in 5.68 seconds =================
```

The `-ra` flag can be passed to produce a nice summary with the full name of all failing tests at the end of the session:

```
. . .
_____ test_type_checking _____

    def test_type_checking():
>       assert 0
E       assert 0

tests\core\test_core.py:12: AssertionError
======================= short test summary info ========================
FAIL tests\test_assert_demo.py::test_approx_simple_fail
FAIL tests\test_assert_demo.py::test_approx_list_fail
FAIL tests\test_assert_demo.py::test_default_health
FAIL tests\test_assert_demo.py::test_default_player_class
FAIL tests\test_assert_demo.py::test_warrior_short_description
FAIL tests\test_assert_demo.py::test_warrior_long_description
FAIL tests\test_assert_demo.py::test_get_starting_equiment
FAIL tests\test_assert_demo.py::test_long_list
FAIL tests\test_assert_demo.py::test_starting_health
FAIL tests\test_assert_demo.py::test_player_classes
FAIL tests\test_checks.py::test_invalid_class_name
FAIL tests\test_read_properties.py::test_read_properties
FAIL tests\core\test_core.py::test_check_options
FAIL tests\core\test_core.py::test_type_checking
================ 14 failed, 17 passed in 5.68 seconds =================
```

This flag is particularly useful when running the suite from the command line directly, because scrolling the terminal to find out which tests failed can be annoying.

The flag is actually `-r`, which accepts a number of single-character arguments:

- f (failed): `assert` failed
- e (error): raised an unexpected exception
- s (skipped): skipped (we will get to this in the next chapter)
- x (xfailed): expected to fail, did fail (we will get to this in the next chapter)
- X (xpassed): expected to fail, but passed (!) (we will get to this in the next chapter)
- p (passed): test passed
- P (passed with output): displays captured output even for passing tests (careful – this usually produces a lot of output)
- a: shows all the above, except for P; this is the **default** and is usually the most useful.

The flag can receive any combination of the above. So, for example, if you are interested in failures and errors only, you can pass `-rfe` to pytest.

In general, I recommend sticking with `-ra`, without thinking too much about it and you will obtain the most benefits.

Configuration: pytest.ini

Users can customize some pytest behavior using a configuration file called `pytest.ini`. This file is usually placed at the root of the repository and contains a number of configuration values that are applied to all test runs for that project. It is meant to be kept under version control and committed with the rest of the code.

The format follows a simple ini-style format with all pytest-related options under a `[pytest]` section. For more details, go to:`https://docs.python.org/3/library/configparser.html`.

    [pytest]

The location of this file also defines what pytest calls the **root directory** (`rootdir`): if present, the directory that contains the configuration file is considered the root directory.

The root directory is used for the following:

- To create the tests node IDs
- As a stable location to store information about the project (by pytest plugins and features)

Without the configuration file, the root directory will depend on which directory you execute pytest from and which arguments are passed (the description of the algorithm can be found here: `https://docs.pytest.org/en/latest/customize.html#finding-the-rootdir`). For this reason, it is always recommended to have a `pytest.ini` file in all but the simplest projects, even if empty.

 Always define a `pytest.ini` file, even if empty.

If you are using `tox`, you can put a `[pytest]` section in the traditional `tox.ini` file and it will work just as well. For more details, go to: `https://tox.readthedocs.io/en/latest/`:

```
[tox]
envlist = py27,py36
...

[pytest]
# pytest options
```

This is useful to avoid cluttering your repository root with too many files, but it is really a matter of preference.

Now, we will take a look at more common configuration options. More options will be introduced in the coming chapters as we cover new features.

Additional command-line: addopts

We learned some very useful command-line options. Some of them might become personal favorites, but having to type them all the time would be annoying.

The `addopts` configuration option can be used instead to always add a set of options to the command line:

```
[pytest]
addopts=--tb=native --maxfail=10 -v
```

With that configuration, typing the following:

λ **pytest tests/test_core.py**

Is the same as typing:

λ **pytest --tb=native --max-fail=10 -v tests/test_core.py**

Note that, despite its name, `addopts` actually inserts the options **before** other options typed in the command line. This makes it possible to override most options in `addopts` when passing them in explicitly.

For example, the following code will now display **auto** tracebacks, instead of native ones, as configured in `pytest.ini`:

λ **pytest --tb=auto tests/test_core.py**

Customizing a collection

By default, pytest collects tests using this heuristic:

- Files that match test_*.py and *_test.py
- Inside test modules, functions that match test* and classes that match Test*
- Inside test classes, methods that match test*

This convention is simple to understand and works for most projects, but they can be overwritten by these configuration options:

- python_files: a list of patterns to use to collect test modules
- python_functions: a list of patterns to use to collect test functions and test methods
- python_classes: a list of patterns to use to collect test classes

Here's an example of a configuration file changing the defaults:

```
[pytest]
python_files = unittests_*.py
python_functions = check_*
python_classes = *TestSuite
```

The recommendation is to only use these configuration options for legacy projects that follow a different convention, and stick with the defaults for new projects. Using the defaults is less work and avoids confusing other collaborators.

Cache directory: cache_dir

The --lf and --ff options shown previously are provided by an internal plugin named cacheprovider, which saves data on a directory on disk so it can be accessed in future sessions. This directory by default is located in the **root directory** under the name .pytest_cache. This directory should never be committed to version control.

If you would like to change the location of that directory, you can use the cache_dir option. This option also expands environment variables automatically:

```
[pytest]
cache_dir=$TMP/pytest-cache
```

Avoid recursing into directories: norecursedirs

pytest by default will recurse over all subdirectories of the arguments given on the command line. This might make test collection take more time than desired when recursing into directories that never contain any tests, for example:

- virtualenvs
- Build artifacts
- Documentation
- Version control directories

pytest by default tries to be smart and will not recurse inside folders with the patterns `.*`, `build`, `dist`, `CVS`, `_darcs`, `{arch}`, `*.egg`, `venv`. It also tries to detect virtualenvs automatically by looking at known locations for activation scripts.

The `norecursedirs` option can be used to override the default list of pattern names that pytest should never recurse into:

```
[pytest]
norecursedirs = artifacts _build docs
```

You can also use the `--collect-in-virtualenv` flag to skip the `virtualenv` detection.

In general, users have little need to override the defaults, but if you find yourself adding the same directory over and over again in your projects, consider opening an issue. For more details (`https://github.com/pytest-dev/pytest/issues/new`).

Pick the right place by default: testpaths

As discussed previously, a common directory structure is *out-of-source layout*, with tests separated from the application/library code in a `tests` or similarly named directory. In that layout it is useful to use the `testpaths` configuration option:

```
[pytest]
testpaths = tests
```

This will tell pytest where to look for tests when no files, directories, or node ids are given in the command line, which might speed up test collection. Note that you can configure more than one directory, separated by spaces.

Override options with -o/--override

Finally, a little known feature is that you can override any configuration option directly in the command-line using the -o /--override flags. This flag can be passed multiple times to override more than one option:

```
λ pytest -o python_classes=Suite -o cache_dir=$TMP/pytest-cache
```

Summary

In this chapter, we covered how to use virtualenv and pip to install pytest. After that, we jumped into how to write tests, and the different ways to run them so that we can execute just the tests we are interested in. We had an overview of how pytest can provide rich output information for failing tests for different built-in data types. We learned how to use pytest.raises and pytest.warns to check exceptions and warnings, and pytest.approx to avoid common pitfalls when comparing floating point numbers. Then, we briefly discussed how to organize test files and modules in your projects. We also took a look at some of the more useful command-line options so that we can get productive right away. Finally, we covered how pytest.ini files are used for persistent command-line options and other configuration.

In the next chapter, we will learn how to use marks to help us skip tests on certain platforms, how to let our test suite know when a bug is fixed in our code or in external libraries, and how to group sets of tests so that we can execute them selectively in the command line. After that, we will learn how to apply the same checks to different sets of data to avoid copying and pasting testing code.

Markers and Parametrization

3

After learning the basics of writing and running tests, we will delve into two important pytest features: **marks** and **parametrization**.

Firstly, we will learn about marks, which allow us to selectively run tests based on applied marks, and to attach general data to test functions, which can be used by fixtures and plugins. In the same topic, we will take a look at built-in marks and what they have to offer.

Secondly, we will learn about **test parametrization**, which allows us to easily apply the same test function to a set of input values. This greatly avoids duplicating test code and makes it easy to add new test cases that may appear as our software evolves.

In summary, here is what we will be covering in this chapter:

- Mark basics
- Built-in marks
- Parametrization

Mark basics

Pytest allows you to mark functions and classes with metadata. This metadata can be used to selectively run tests, and is also available for fixtures and plugins, to perform different tasks. Let's take a look at how to create and apply marks to test functions, and later on jump into built-in pytest marks.

Creating marks

Marks are created with the `@pytest.mark` decorator. It works as a factory, so any access to it will automatically create a new mark and apply it to a function. This is easier to understand with an example:

```
@pytest.mark.slow
def test_long_computation():
    ...
```

By using the `@pytest.mark.slow` decorator, you are applying a mark named `slow` to `test_long_computation`.

Marks can also receive **parameters**:

```
@pytest.mark.timeout(10, method="thread")
def test_topology_sort():
    ...
```

The `@pytest.mark.timeout` used in the last example was taken from the pytest-timeout plugin; for more details go to `https://pypi.org/project/pytest-timeout/`. With this, we define that `test_topology_sort` should not take more than 10 seconds, in which case it should be terminated using the `thread` method. Assigning arguments to marks is a very powerful feature, providing plugins and fixtures with a lot of flexibility. We will explore those capabilities and the `pytest-timeout` plugin in the next chapters.

You can add more than one mark to a test by applying the `@pytest.mark` decorator multiple times— for example:

```
@pytest.mark.slow
@pytest.mark.timeout(10, method="thread")
def test_topology_sort():
    ...
```

If you are applying the same mark over and over, you can avoid repeating yourself by assigning it to a variable once and applying it over tests as needed:

```
timeout10 = pytest.mark.timeout(10, method="thread")

@timeout10
def test_topology_sort():
    ...

@timeout10
def test_remove_duplicate_points():
    ...
```

If this mark is used in several tests, you can move it to a testing utility module and import it as needed:

```
from mylib.testing import timeout10

@timeout10
def test_topology_sort():
    ...

@timeout10
def test_remove_duplicate_points():
    ...
```

Running tests based on marks

You can run tests by using marks as selection factors with the −m flag. For example, to run all tests with the slow mark:

```
λ pytest −m slow
```

The −m flag also accepts expressions, so you can do a more advanced selection. To run all tests with the slow mark but not the tests with the serial mark you can use::

```
λ pytest −m "slow and not serial"
```

The expression is limited to the and, not, and or operators.

Custom marks can be useful for optimizing test runs on your CI system. Oftentimes, environment problems, missing dependencies, or even some code committed by mistake might cause the entire test suite to fail. By using marks, you can choose a few tests that are fast and/or broad enough to detect problems in a good portion of the code and then run those first, before all the other tests. If any of those tests fail, we abort the job and avoid wasting potentially a lot of time by running all tests that are doomed to fail anyway.

We start by applying a custom mark to those tests. Any name will do, but a common name used is smoke, as in *smoke detector*, to detect problems before everything bursts into flames.

You then run smoke tests first, and only after they pass do, you run the complete test suite:

```
λ pytest −m "smoke"
...
λ pytest −m "not smoke"
```

If any smoke test fails, you don't have to wait for the entire suite to finish to obtain this feedback.

You can add to this technique by creating layers of tests, from simplest to slowest, creating a test hierarchy of sorts. For example:

- smoke
- unittest
- integration
- <all the rest>

This would then be executed like this:

```
λ pytest -m "smoke"
...
λ pytest -m "unittest"
...
λ pytest -m "integration"
...
λ pytest -m "not smoke and not unittest and not integration"
```

Make sure to include the fourth step; otherwise, tests without marks will never run.

Using marks to differentiate tests in different pytest runs can also be used in other scenarios. For instance, when using the `pytest-xdist` plugin to run tests in parallel, we have a parallel session that executes most test suites in parallel but might decide to run a few tests in a separate pytest session serially because they are sensitive or problematic when executed together.

Applying marks to classes

You can apply the `@pytest.mark` decorator to a class. This will apply that same mark to all tests methods in that class, avoiding have to copy and paste the mark code over all test methods:

```
@pytest.mark.timeout(10)
class TestCore:

    def test_simple_simulation(self):
        ...

    def test_compute_tracers(self):
        ...
```

The previous code is essentially the same as the following code:

```
class TestCore:
```

```
@pytest.mark.timeout(10)
def test_simple_simulation(self):
    ...

@pytest.mark.timeout(10)
def test_compute_tracers(self):
    ...
```

However, there is one difference: applying the @pytest.mark decorator to a class means that all its subclasses will inherit the mark. Subclassing test classes is not common, but it is sometimes a useful technique to avoid repeating test code, or to ensure that implementations comply with a certain interface. We will see more examples of this later in this chapter and in Chapter 4, *Fixtures*.

Like test functions, decorators can be applied multiple times:

```
@pytest.mark.slow
@pytest.mark.timeout(10)
class TestCore:

    def test_simple_simulation(self):
        ...

    def test_compute_tracers(self):
        ...
```

Applying marks to modules

We can also apply a mark to all test functions and test classes in a module. Just declare a **global variable** named pytestmark:

```
import pytest

pytestmark = pytest.mark.timeout(10)


class TestCore:

    def test_simple_simulation(self):
        ...


def test_compute_tracers():
    ...
```

The following is the equivalent to this:

```
import pytest


@pytest.mark.timeout(10)
class TestCore:

    def test_simple_simulation(self):
        ...


@pytest.mark.timeout(10)
def test_compute_tracers():
    ...
```

You can use a `tuple` or `list` of marks to apply multiple marks as well:

```
import pytest

pytestmark = [pytest.mark.slow, pytest.mark.timeout(10)]
```

Custom marks and pytest.ini

Being able to declare new marks on the fly just by applying the `pytest.mark` decorator is convenient. It makes it a breeze to quickly start enjoying the benefits of using marks.

This convenience comes at a price: it is possible for a user to make a typo in the mark name, for example `@pytest.mark.solw`, instead of `@pytest.mark.slow`. Depending on the project under testing, this typo might be a mere annoyance or a more serious problem.

So, let's go back to our previous example, where a test suite is executed in layers on CI based on marked tests:

- smoke
- unittest
- integration
- <all the rest>

```
λ pytest -m "smoke"
...
λ pytest -m "unittest"
...
λ pytest -m "integration"
```

```
  . . .
λ pytest -m "not smoke and not unittest and not integration"
```

A developer could make a typo while applying a mark to one of the tests:

```
@pytest.mark.smoek
def test_simulation_setup():
    . . .
```

This means the test will execute at the last step, instead of on the first step with the other smoke tests. Again, this might vary from a small nuisance to a terrible problem, depending on the test suite.

Mature test suites that have a fixed set of marks might declare them in the pytest.ini file:

```
[pytest]
markers =
    slow
    serial
    smoke: quick tests that cover a good portion of the code
    unittest: unit tests for basic functionality
    integration: cover to cover functionality testing
```

The markers option accepts a list of markers in the form of <name>: description, with the description part being optional (slow and serial in the last example don't have a description).

A full list of marks can be displayed by using the --markers flag:

```
λ pytest --markers
@pytest.mark.slow:

@pytest.mark.serial:

@pytest.mark.smoke: quick tests that cover a good portion of the code

@pytest.mark.unittest: unit tests for basic functionality

@pytest.mark.integration: cover to cover functionality testing

  . . .
```

The --strict flag makes it an error to use marks not declared in the pytest.ini file. Using our previous example with a typo, we now obtain an error, instead of pytest silently creating the mark when running with --strict:

```
λ pytest --strict tests\test_wrong_mark.py
```

```
...
collected 0 items / 1 errors

============================== ERRORS ================================
_____ ERROR collecting tests/test_wrong_mark.py _____
tests\test_wrong_mark.py:4: in <module>
    @pytest.mark.smoek
..\..\.env36\lib\site-packages\_pytest\mark\structures.py:311: in
__getattr__
    self._check(name)
..\..\.env36\lib\site-packages\_pytest\mark\structures.py:327: in _check
    raise AttributeError("%r not a registered marker" % (name,))
E AttributeError: 'smoek' not a registered marker
!!!!!!!!!!!!!!! Interrupted: 1 errors during collection !!!!!!!!!!!!!!!
======================= 1 error in 0.09 seconds =======================
```

Test suites that want to ensure that all marks are registered in `pytest.ini` should also use `addopts`:

```
[pytest]
addopts = --strict
markers =
    slow
    serial
    smoke: quick tests that cover a good portion of the code
    unittest: unit tests for basic functionality
    integration: cover to cover functionality testing
```

Built-in marks

Having learned the basics of marks and how to use them, let's now take a look at some built-in pytest marks. This is not an exhaustive list of all built-in marks, but the more commonly used ones. Also, keep in mind that many plugins introduce other marks as well.

@pytest.mark.skipif

You might have tests that should not be executed unless some condition is met. For example, some tests might depend on certain libraries that are not always installed, or a local database that might not be online, or are executed only on certain platforms.

Pytest provides a built-in mark, `skipif`, that can be used to *skip* tests based on specific conditions. Skipped tests are not executed if the condition is true, and are not counted towards test suite failures.

For example, you can use the `skipif` mark to always skip a test when executing on Windows:

```
import sys
import pytest

@pytest.mark.skipif(
    sys.platform.startswith("win"),
    reason="fork not available on Windows",
)
def test_spawn_server_using_fork():
    ...
```

The first argument to `@pytest.mark.skipif` is the condition: in this example, we are telling pytest to skip this test in Windows. The `reason=` keyword argument is mandatory and is used to display why the test was skipped when using the `-ra` flag:

```
tests\test_skipif.py s                                    [100%]
====================== short test summary info =======================
SKIP [1] tests\test_skipif.py:6: fork not available on Windows
==================== 1 skipped in 0.02 seconds =======================
```

It is good style to always write descriptive messages, including ticket numbers when applicable.

Alternatively, we can write the same condition as follows:

```
import os
import pytest

@pytest.mark.skipif(
    not hasattr(os, 'fork'), reason="os.fork not available"
)
def test_spawn_server_using_fork2():
    ...
```

The latter version checks whether the actual feature is available, instead of making assumptions based on the platform (Windows currently does not have an `os.fork` function, but perhaps in the future Windows might support the function). The same thing is common when testing features of libraries based on their version, instead of checking whether some functions exist. I suggest that so this reads: some functions exist. I suggest that when possible, prefer to check whether a function actually exists, instead of checking for a specific version of the library.

Checking capabilities and features is usually a better approach, instead of checking platforms and library version numbers.

The following is the full `@pytest.mark.skipif` signature:

```
@pytest.mark.skipif(condition, *, reason=None)
```

pytest.skip

The `@pytest.mark.skipif` decorator is very handy, but the mark must evaluate the condition at `import/collection` time, to determine whether the test should be skipped. We want to minimize test collection time, because, after all, we might end up not even executing all tests if the `-k` or `--lf` flags are being used, for example.

Sometimes, it might even be almost impossible (without some gruesome hack) to check whether a test should be skipped during import time. For example, you can make the decision to skip a test based on the capabilities of the graphics driver only after initializing the underlying graphics library, and initializing the graphics subsystem is definitely not something you want to do at import time.

For those cases, pytest lets you skip tests imperatively in the test body by using the `pytest.skip` function:

```
def test_shaders():
    initialize_graphics()
    if not supports_shaders():
        pytest.skip("shades not supported in this driver")
    # rest of the test code
    ...
```

`pytest.skip` works by raising an internal exception, so it follows normal Python exception semantics, and nothing else needs to be done for the test to be skipped properly.

pytest.importorskip

It is common for libraries to have tests that depend on a certain library being installed. For example, pytest's own test suite has some tests for `numpy` arrays, which should be skipped if `numpy` is not installed.

One way to handle this would be to manually try to import the library and skip the test if it is not present:

```
def test_tracers_as_arrays_manual():
    try:
        import numpy
    except ImportError:
        pytest.skip("requires numpy")
    ...
```

This can get old quickly, so for this reason, pytest provides the handy `pytest.importorskip` function:

```
def test_tracers_as_arrays():
    numpy = pytest.importorskip("numpy")
    ...
```

`pytest.importorskip` will import the module and return the module object, or skip the test entirely if the module could not be imported.

If your test requires a minimum version of the library, `pytest.importorskip` also supports a `minversion` argument:

```
def test_tracers_as_arrays_114():
    numpy = pytest.importorskip("numpy", minversion="1.14")
    ...
```

@pytest.mark.xfail

You can use `@pytest.mark.xfail` decorator to indicate that a test is `expected to fail`. As usual, we apply the mark decorator to the test function or method:

```
@pytest.mark.xfail
def test_simulation_34():
    ...
```

This mark supports some parameters, all of which we will see later in this section; but one in particular warrants discussion now: the `strict` parameter. This parameter defines two distinct behaviors for the mark:

- With `strict=False` (the default), the test will be counted separately as an **XPASS** (if it passes) or an **XFAIL** (if it fails), and will **not fail the test suite**
- With `strict=True`, the test will be marked as **XFAIL** if it fails, but if it unexpectedly passes, it will **fail the test suite**, as a normal failing test would

But why would you want to write a test that you expect to fail anyway, and in which occasions is this useful? This might seem weird at first, but there are a few situations where this comes in handy.

The first situation is when a test always fails, and you want to be told (loudly) if it suddenly starts passing. This can happen when:

- You found out that the cause of a bug in your code is due to a problem in a third-party library. In this situation, you can write a failing test that demonstrates the problem, and mark it with `@pytest.mark.xfail(strict=True)`. If the test fails, the test will be marked as **XFAIL** in the test session summary, but if the test **passes**, it will **fail the test suite**. This test might start to pass when you upgrade the library that was causing the problem, and this will alert you that the issue has been fixed and needs your attention.
- You have thought about a new feature, and design one or more test cases that exercise it even before your start implementing it. You can commit the tests with the `@pytest.mark.xfail(strict=True)` mark applied, and remove the mark from the tests as you code the new feature. This is very useful in a collaborative environment, where one person supplies tests on how they envision a new feature/API, and another person implements it based on the test cases.
- You discover a bug in your application and write a test case demonstrating the problem. You might not have the time to tackle it right now or another person would be better suited to work in that part of the code. In this situation, marking the test as `@pytest.mark.xfail(strict=True)` would be a good approach.

All the cases above share one characteristic: you have a failing test and want to know whether it suddenly starts passing. In this case, the fact that the test passes warns you about a fact that requires your attention: a new version of a library with a bug fix has been released, part of a feature is now working as intended, or a known bug has been fixed.

The other situation where the `xfail` mark is useful is when you have tests that fail *sometimes*, also called **flaky tests**. Flaky tests are tests that fail on occasion, even if the underlying code has not changed. There are many reasons why tests fail in a way that appears to be random; the following are a few:

- Timing issues in multi threaded code
- Intermittent network connectivity problems
- Tests that don't deal with asynchronous events correctly
- Relying on non-deterministic behavior

That is just to list a few possible causes. This non-determinism usually happens in tests with broader scopes, such as integration or UI. The fact is that you will almost always have to deal with flaky tests in large test suites.

Flaky tests are a serious problem, because the test suite is supposed to be an indicator that the code is working as intended and that it can detect real problems when they happen. Flaky tests destroy that image, because often developers will see flaky tests failing that don't have anything to do with recent code changes. When this becomes commonplace, people begin to just run the test suite again in the hope that this time the flaky test passes (and it often does), but this erodes the trust in the test suite as a whole, and brings frustration to the development team. You should treat flaky tests as a menace that should be contained and dealt with.

Here are some suggestions regarding how to deal with flaky tests within a development team:

1. First, you need to be able to correctly identify flaky tests. If a test fails that apparently doesn't have anything to do with the recent changes, run the tests again. If the test that failed previously now `passes`, it means the test is flaky.
2. Create an issue to deal with that particular flaky test in your ticket system. Use a naming convention or other means to label that issue as related to a flaky test (for example GitHub or JIRA labels).
3. Apply the `@pytest.mark.xfail(reason="flaky test #123", strict=False)` mark, making sure to include the issue ticket number or identifier. Feel free to add more information to the description, if you like.
4. Make sure to periodically assign issues about flaky tests to yourself or other team members (for example, during sprint planning). The idea is to take care of flaky tests at a comfortable pace, eventually reducing or eliminating them altogether.

These practices take care of two major problems: they allow you to avoid eroding trust in the test suite, by getting flaky tests out of the way of the development team, and they put a policy in place to deal with flaky tests in their due time.

Having covered the situations where the `xfail` mark is useful, let's take a look at the full signature:

```
@pytest.mark.xfail(condition=None, *, reason=None, raises=None, run=True,
strict=False)
```

- condition: the first parameter, if given, is a `True/False` condition, similar to the one used by `@pytest.mark.skipif`: if `False`, the `xfail` mark is ignored. It is useful to mark a test as `xfail` based on an external condition, such as the platform, Python version, library version, and so on.

  - ```
    @pytest.mark.xfail(
        sys.platform.startswith("win"),
        reason="flaky on Windows #42", strict=False
    )
    def test_login_dialog():
        ...
    ```

- reason: a string that will be shown in the short test summary when the `-ra` flag is used. It is highly recommended to always use this parameter to explain the reason why the test has been marked as `xfail` and/or include a ticket number.

  - ```
    @pytest.mark.xfail(
        sys.platform.startswith("win"),
        reason="flaky on Windows #42", strict=False
    )
    def test_login_dialog():
        ...
    ```

- raises: given an exception type, it declares that we expect the test to raise an instance of that exception. If the test raises another type of exception (even `AssertionError`), the test will `fail` normally. It is especially useful for missing functionality or to test for known bugs.

  - ```
    @pytest.mark.xfail(raises=NotImplementedError,
                       reason='will be implemented in #987')
    def test_credential_check():
        check_credentials('Hawkwood') # not implemented yet
    ```

- run: if `False`, the test will not even be executed and will fail as XFAIL. This is particularly useful for tests that run code that might crash the test-suite process (for example, C/C++ extensions causing a segmentation fault due to a known problem).

  - ```
    @pytest.mark.xfail(
        run=False, reason="undefined particles cause a crash #625"
    )
    def test_undefined_particle_collision_crash():
        collide(Particle(), Particle())
    ```

- strict: if True, a passing test will fail the test suite. If False, the test will not fail the test suite regardless of the outcome (the default is False). This was discussed in detail at the start of this section.

The configuration variable xfail_strict controls the default value of the strict parameter of xfail marks:

```
[pytest]
xfail_strict = True
```

Setting it to True means that all xfail-marked tests without an explicit strict parameter are considered an actual failure expectation instead of a flaky test. Any xfail mark that explicitly passes the strict parameter overrides the configuration value.

pytest.xfail

Finally, you can imperatively trigger an XFAIL result within a test by calling the pytest.xfail function:

```
def test_particle_splitting():
    initialize_physics()
    import numpy
    if numpy.__version__ < "1.13":
        pytest.xfail("split computation fails with numpy < 1.13")
    ...
```

Similar to pytest.skip, this is useful when you can only determine whether you need to mark a test as xfail at runtime.

Parametrization

A common testing activity is passing multiple values to the same test function and asserting the outcome.

Suppose we have an application that allows the user to define custom mathematical formulas, which will be parsed and evaluated at runtime. The formulas are given as strings, and can make use of mathematical functions such as sin, cos, log, and so on. A very simple way to implement this in Python would be to use the eval built-in (https://docs.python.org/3/library/functions.html#eval), but because it can execute arbitrary code, we opt to use a custom tokenizer and evaluator for safety, instead..

Let's not delve into the implementation details but rather focus on a test:

```python
def test_formula_parsing():
    tokenizer = FormulaTokenizer()
    formula = Formula.from_string("C0 * x + 10", tokenizer)
    assert formula.eval(x=1.0, C0=2.0) == pytest.approx(12.0)
```

Here, we create a `Tokenizer` class, which is used by our implementation to break the formula string into internal tokens for later processing. Then, we pass the formula string and tokenizer to `Formula.from_string`, to obtain a formula object. With the formula object on our hands, we pass the input values to `formula.eval` and check that the returned value matches our expectation.

But we also want to test other math operations, to ensure we are covering all the features of our `Formula` class.

One approach is to expand our test by using multiple assertions to check other formulas and input values:

```python
def test_formula_parsing():
    tokenizer = FormulaTokenizer()
    formula = Formula.from_string("C0 * x + 10", tokenizer)
    assert formula.eval(x=1.0, C0=2.0) == pytest.approx(12.0)

    formula = Formula.from_string("sin(x) + 2 * cos(x)", tokenizer)
    assert formula.eval(x=0.7) == pytest.approx(2.1739021)

    formula = Formula.from_string("log(x) + 3", tokenizer)
    assert formula.eval(x=2.71828182846) == pytest.approx(4.0)
```

This works, but if one of the assertions fails, the following assertions within the test function will not be executed. If there are multiple failures, we will have to run the test multiple times to see all of them and eventually fix all the issues.

To see multiple failures per test run, we might decide to explicitly write a separate test for each assertion:

```python
def test_formula_linear():
    tokenizer = FormulaTokenizer()
    formula = Formula.from_string("C0 * x + 10", tokenizer)
    assert formula.eval(x=1.0, C0=2.0) == pytest.approx(12.0)

def test_formula_sin_cos():
    tokenizer = FormulaTokenizer()
    formula = Formula.from_string("sin(x) + 2 * cos(x)", tokenizer)
    assert formula.eval(x=0.7) == pytest.approx(2.1739021)
```

```
def test_formula_log():
    tokenizer = FormulaTokenizer()
    formula = Formula.from_string("log(x) + 3", tokenizer)
    assert formula.eval(x=2.71828182846) == pytest.approx(4.0)
```

But now we are duplicating code all over the place, which will make maintenance more difficult. Suppose in the future `FormulaTokenizer` is updated to explicitly receive a list of functions that can be used in formulas. This means that we would have to update the creation of `FormulaTokenzier` in several places.

To avoid repeating ourselves, we might decide to write this instead:

```
def test_formula_parsing2():
    values = [
        ("C0 * x + 10", dict(x=1.0, C0=2.0), 12.0),
        ("sin(x) + 2 * cos(x)", dict(x=0.7), 2.1739021),
        ("log(x) + 3", dict(x=2.71828182846), 4.0),
    ]
    tokenizer = FormulaTokenizer()
    for formula, inputs, result in values:
        formula = Formula.from_string(formula, tokenizer)
        assert formula.eval(**inputs) == pytest.approx(result)
```

This solves the problem of duplicating code, but now we are back to the initial problem of seeing only one failure at a time.

Enter @pytest.mark.parametrize

To solve all the above problems, pytest provides the much-loved `@pytest.mark.parametrize` mark. With this mark, you are able to provide a list of input values to the test, and pytest automatically generates multiple test functions for each input value.

The following shows this in action:

```
@pytest.mark.parametrize(
    "formula, inputs, result",
    [
        ("C0 * x + 10", dict(x=1.0, C0=2.0), 12.0),
        ("sin(x) + 2 * cos(x)", dict(x=0.7), 2.1739021),
        ("log(x) + 3", dict(x=2.71828182846), 4.0),
    ],
)
def test_formula_parsing(formula, inputs, result):
    tokenizer = FormulaTokenizer()
```

```
formula = Formula.from_string(formula, tokenizer)
assert formula.eval(**inputs) == pytest.approx(result)
```

The `@pytest.mark.parametrize` mark automatically generates multiple test functions, parametrizing them with the arguments given to the mark. The call receives two parameters:

- `argnames`: a comma-separated string of argument names that will be passed to the test function.
- `argvalues`: a sequence of tuples, with each tuple generating a new test invocation. Each item in the tuple corresponds to an argument name, so the first tuple (`"C0 * x + 10", dict(x=1.0, C0=2.0), 12.0`) will generate a call to the test function with the arguments:
  - `formula = "C0 * x + 10"`
  - `inputs = dict(x=1.0, C0=2.0)`
  - `expected = 12.0`

Using this mark, pytest will run `test_formula_parsing` three times, passing one set of arguments given by the `argvalues` parameter each time. It will also automatically generate a different node ID for each test, making it easy to distinguish between them:

```
======================== test session starts ==========================
...
collected 8 items / 5 deselected

test_formula.py::test_formula[C0 * x + 10-inputs0-12.0]
test_formula.py::test_formula[sin(x) + 2 * cos(x)-inputs1-2.1739021]
test_formula.py::test_formula[log(x) + 3-inputs2-4.0]
============== 3 passed, 5 deselected in 0.05 seconds ===============
```

It is also important to note that the body of the function is just as compact as our starting test at the beginning of this section, but now we have multiple tests which allows us to see multiple failures when they happen.

Test parametrization not only avoids repeating test code and makes maintenance easier, it also invites you and the next developer who comes along to add more input values as the code matures. It encourages developers to cover more cases, because people are more eager to add a single line to the `argvalues` of a parametrized test than to copy and paste an entire new test to cover another input value.

In summary, `@pytest.mark.parametrize` will make you cover more input cases, with very little overhead. It is definitely a very useful feature and should be used whenever you have multiple input values to be tested in the same way.

Applying marks to value sets

Often, in parametrized tests, you find the need to apply one or more marks to a set of parameters as you would to a normal test function. For example, you want to apply a `timeout` mark to one set of parameters because it takes too long to run, or `xfail` a set of parameters, because it has not been implemented yet.

In those cases, use `pytest.param` to wrap the set of values and apply the marks you want:

```
@pytest.mark.parametrize(
    "formula, inputs, result",
    [
        ...
        ("log(x) + 3", dict(x=2.71828182846), 4.0),
        pytest.param(
            "hypot(x, y)", dict(x=3, y=4), 5.0,
            marks=pytest.mark.xfail(reason="not implemented: #102"),
        ),
    ],
)
```

The signature of `pytest.param` is this:

```
pytest.param(*values, **kw)
```

Where:

- `*values` is the parameter set: `"hypot(x, y)", dict(x=3, y=4), 5.0`.
- `**kw` are options as keyword arguments: `marks=pytest.mark.xfail(reason="not implemented: #102")`. It accepts a single mark or a sequence of marks. There is another option, `ids`, which will be shown in the next section.

Behind the scenes, every tuple of parameters passed to `@pytest.mark.parametrize` is converted to a `pytest.param` without extra options, so, for example, in the following the first code snippet is equivalent to the second code snippet:

```
@pytest.mark.parametrize(
    "formula, inputs, result",
    [
        ("C0 * x + 10", dict(x=1.0, C0=2.0), 12.0),
        ("sin(x) + 2 * cos(x)", dict(x=0.7), 2.1739021),
    ]
)

@pytest.mark.parametrize(
```

```
        "formula, inputs, result",
        [
            pytest.param("C0 * x + 10", dict(x=1.0, C0=2.0), 12.0),
            pytest.param("sin(x) + 2 * cos(x)", dict(x=0.7), 2.1739021),
        ]
    )
```

Customizing test IDs

Consider this example:

```
@pytest.mark.parametrize(
    "formula, inputs, result",
    [
        ("x + 3", dict(x=1.0), 4.0,),
        ("x - 1", dict(x=6.0), 5.0,),
    ],
)
def test_formula_simple(formula, inputs, result):
    ...
```

As we have seen, pytest automatically creates custom test IDs, based on the parameters used in a parametrized call. Running `pytest -v` will generate these test IDs:

```
======================= test session starts =======================
...
tests/test_formula.py::test_formula_simple[x + 3-inputs0-4.0]
tests/test_formula.py::test_formula_simple[x - 1-inputs1-5.0]
```

If you don't like the automatically generated IDs, you can use `pytest.param` and the `id` option to customize it:

```
@pytest.mark.parametrize(
    "formula, inputs, result",
    [
        pytest.param("x + 3", dict(x=1.0), 4.0, id='add'),
        pytest.param("x - 1", dict(x=6.0), 5.0, id='sub'),
    ],
)
def test_formula_simple(formula, inputs, result):
    ...
```

This produces the following:

```
======================= test session starts =======================
...
tests/test_formula.py::test_formula_simple[add]
```

```
tests/test_formula.py::test_formula_simple[sub]
```

This is also useful because it makes selecting tests significantly easier when using the –k flag:

```
λ pytest -k "x + 3-inputs0-4.0"
```

versus:

```
λ pytest -k "add"
```

Testing multiple implementations

Well-designed systems usually make use of abstractions provided by interfaces, instead of being tied to specific implementations. This makes a system more resilient to future changes because, to extend it, you need to implement a new extension that complies with the expected interface, and integrate it into the system.

One challenge that often comes up is how to make sure existing implementations comply with all the details of a specific interface.

For example, suppose our system needs to be able to serialize some internal classes into a text format to save and load to disk. The following are some of the internal classes in our system:

- Quantity: represents a value and a unit of measure. For example Quantity(10, "m") means *10 meters*. Quantity objects have addition, subtraction, and multiplication—basically, all the operators that you would expect from a native float, but taking the unit of measure into account.
- Pipe: represents a duct where some fluid can flow through. It has a length and diameter, both Quantity instances.

Initially, in our development, we only need to save those objects in **JSON** format, so we go ahead and implement a straightforward serializer class, that is able to serialize and de-serialize our classes:

```
class JSONSerializer:

    def serialize_quantity(self, quantity: Quantity) -> str:
        ...

    def deserialize_quantity(self, data: str) -> Quantity:
        ...
```

```
def serialize_pipe(self, pipe: Pipe) -> str:
    ...

def deserialize_pipe(self, data: str) -> Pipe:
    ...
```

Now we should write some tests to ensure everything is working:

```
class Test:

    def test_quantity(self):
        serializer = JSONSerializer()
        quantity = Quantity(10, "m")
        data = serializer.serialize(quantity)
        new_quantity = serializer.deserialize(data)
        assert new_quantity == quantity

    def test_pipe(self):
        serializer = JSONSerializer()
        pipe = Pipe(
            length=Quantity(1000, "m"), diameter=Quantity(35, "cm")
        )
        data = serializer.serialize(pipe)
        new_pipe = serializer.deserialize(data)
        assert new_pipe == pipe
```

This works well and is a perfectly valid approach, given our requirements.

Some time passes, and new requirements arrive: now we need to serialize our objects into other formats, namely XML and YAML (http://yaml.org/). To keep things simple, we create two new classes, XMLSerializer and YAMLSerializer, which implement the same serialize/deserialize methods. Because they comply with the same interface as JSONSerializer, we can use the new classes interchangeably in our system, which is great.

But how do we test the different implementations?

A naive approach would be to loop over the different implementations inside each test:

```
class Test:

    def test_quantity(self):
        for serializer in [
            JSONSerializer(), XMLSerializer(), YAMLSerializer()
        ]:
            quantity = Quantity(10, "m")
            data = serializer.serialize(quantity)
```

```
            new_quantity = serializer.deserialize(data)
            assert new_quantity == quantity

    def test_pipe(self):
        for serializer in [
            JSONSerializer(), XMLSerializer(), YAMLSerializer()
        ]:
            pipe = Pipe(
                length=Quantity(1000, "m"),
                diameter=Quantity(35, "cm"),
            )
            data = serializer.serialize(pipe)
            new_pipe = serializer.deserialize(data)
            assert new_pipe == pipe
```

This works, but it is not ideal, because we have to copy and paste the loop definition in each test, making it harder to maintain. Also, if one of the serializers fails, the next ones in the list will never be executed.

Another, horrible approach, would be to copy and paste the entire test functions, replacing the serializer class each time, but we won't be showing that here.

A much better solution is to use `@pytest.mark.parametrize` at class level. Observe:

```
@pytest.mark.parametrize(
    "serializer_class",
    [JSONSerializer, XMLSerializer, YAMLSerializer],
)
class Test:

    def test_quantity(self, serializer_class):
        serializer = serializer_class()
        quantity = Quantity(10, "m")
        data = serializer.serialize(quantity)
        new_quantity = serializer.deserialize(data)
        assert new_quantity == quantity

    def test_pipe(self, serializer_class):
        serializer = serializer_class()
        pipe = Pipe(
            length=Quantity(1000, "m"), diameter=Quantity(35, "cm")
        )
        data = serializer.serialize(pipe)
        new_pipe = serializer.deserialize(data)
        assert new_pipe == pipe
```

With a small change, we have multiplied our existing tests to cover all the new implementations:

```
test_parametrization.py::Test::test_quantity[JSONSerializer] PASSED
test_parametrization.py::Test::test_quantity[XMLSerializer] PASSED
test_parametrization.py::Test::test_quantity[YAMLSerializer] PASSED
test_parametrization.py::Test::test_pipe[JSONSerializer] PASSED
test_parametrization.py::Test::test_pipe[XMLSerializer] PASSED
test_parametrization.py::Test::test_pipe[YAMLSerializer] PASSED
```

The `@pytest.mark.parametrize` decorator also makes it very clear that new implementations should be added to the list and that all existing tests must pass. New tests added to the class also need to pass for all implementations.

In summary, `@pytest.mark.parametrize` can be a very powerful tool to ensure that different implementations comply with the specifications of an interface.

Summary

In this chapter, we learned how to use marks to organize our code and help us run the test suite in flexible ways. We then looked at how to use the `@pytest.mark.skipif` to conditionally skip tests, and how to use the `@pytest.mark.xfail` mark to deal with expected failures and flaky tests. Then we discussed ways of dealing with flaky tests in a collaborative environment. Finally, we discussed the benefits of using `@pytest.mark.parametrize` to avoid repeating our testing code and to make it easy for ourselves and others to add new input cases to existing tests.

In the next chapter, we will finally get to one of pytest's most loved and powerful features: **fixtures**.

4
Fixtures

In the previous chapter, we learned how to use marks and parametrization effectively to skip tests, mark them as expected to fail, and parameterize them, to avoid repetition.

Tests in the real world often need to create resources or data to work on: a temporary directory to output some files to, a database connection to test the I/O layer of an application, a web server for integration testing. Those are all examples of resources that are required in more complex testing scenarios. More complex resources often need to be cleaned up at the end of the test session: removing a temporary directory, cleaning up and disconnecting from a database, shutting down a web server. Also, these resources should be easily shared across tests, because during testing we often need to reuse a resource for different test scenarios. Some resources are costly to create, but because they are immutable or can be restored to a pristine state, they should be created only once and shared with all the tests that require it, only being destroyed when the last test that needs them finishes.

All of the previous requirements and more are covered by one of the most important of pytest's features: **fixtures**.

Here's what we will cover in this chapter:

- Introducing fixtures
- Sharing fixtures with `conftest.py` files
- Scopes
- Autouse
- Parametrization
- Using marks from fixtures
- An overview of built-in fixtures
- Tips/discussion

Introducing fixtures

Most tests need some kind of data or resource to operate on:

```
def test_highest_rated():
    series = [
        ("The Office", 2005, 8.8),
        ("Scrubs", 2001, 8.4),
        ("IT Crowd", 2006, 8.5),
        ("Parks and Recreation", 2009, 8.6),
        ("Seinfeld", 1989, 8.9),
    ]
    assert highest_rated(series) == "Seinfeld"
```

Here, we have a list of (series name, year, rating) tuples that we use to test the highest_rated function. Inlining data into the test code as we do here works well for isolated tests, but often you have a dataset that can be used by multiple tests. One solution would be to copy over the dataset to each test:

```
def test_highest_rated():
    series = [
        ("The Office", 2005, 8.8),
        ...,
    ]
    assert highest_rated(series) == "Seinfeld"

def test_oldest():
    series = [
        ("The Office", 2005, 8.8),
        ...,
    ]
    assert oldest(series) == "Seinfeld"
```

But this gets old quickly—plus, copying and pasting things around will hurt maintainability in the long run, for example, if the data layout changes (adding a new item to the tuple or the cast size, for example).

Enter fixtures

Pytest's solution to this problem is fixtures. Fixtures are used to provide resources that test the functions and methods we need to execute.

They are created using normal Python functions and the `@pytest.fixture` decorator:

```
@pytest.fixture
def comedy_series():
    return [
        ("The Office", 2005, 8.8),
        ("Scrubs", 2001, 8.4),
        ("IT Crowd", 2006, 8.5),
        ("Parks and Recreation", 2009, 8.6),
        ("Seinfeld", 1989, 8.9),
    ]
```

Here, we are creating a fixture named `comedy_series`, which returns the same list we were using in the previous section.

Tests can access fixtures by declaring the fixture name in their parameter list. The test function then receives the return value of the fixture function as a parameter. Here is the `comedy_series` fixture in action:

```
def test_highest_rated(comedy_series):
    assert highest_rated(comedy_series) == "Seinfeld"

def test_oldest(comedy_series):
    assert oldest(comedy_series) == "Seinfeld"
```

Here's how things work:

- Pytest looks at the test function parameters before calling it. Here, we have one parameter: `comedy_series`.
- For each parameter, pytest gets the fixture function of same name and executes it.
- The return value of each fixture function becomes a named parameter, and the test function is called.

Note that `test_highest_rated` and `test_oldest` each get their own copy of the comedy series list, so they don't risk interfering with each other if they change the list inside the test.

It is also possible to create fixtures in classes using methods:

```
class Test:

    @pytest.fixture
    def drama_series(self):
        return [
            ("The Mentalist", 2008, 8.1),
            ("Game of Thrones", 2011, 9.5),
            ("The Newsroom", 2012, 8.6),
```

```
            ("Cosmos", 1980, 9.3),
        ]
```

Fixtures defined in test classes are only accessible by test methods of the class or subclasses:

```
class Test:
    ...

    def test_highest_rated(self, drama_series):
        assert highest_rated(drama_series) == "Game of Thrones"

    def test_oldest(self, drama_series):
        assert oldest(drama_series) == "Cosmos"
```

Note that test classes might have other non-test methods, like any other class.

Setup/teardown

As we've seen in the introduction, it is very common for resources that are used in testing to require some sort of clean up after a test is done with them.

In our previous example, we had a very small dataset, so inlining it in the fixture was fine. Suppose however that we have a much larger dataset (say, 1,000 entries), so writing it in the code would hurt readability. Often, the dataset is in an external file, for example, in CSV format, so porting it into the Python code is a pain.

A solution to that would be to commit the CSV file containing the series dataset into the repository and read it inside the test, using the built-in `csv` module; for more details go to `https://docs.python.org/3/library/csv.html`.

We can change the `comedy_series` fixture to do just that:

```
@pytest.fixture
def comedy_series():
    file = open("series.csv", "r", newline="")
    return list(csv.reader(file))
```

This works, but we, being diligent developers, want to be able to close that file properly. How can we do that with fixtures?

Fixture clean up is often referred to as **teardown**, and it is easily supported using the `yield` statement:

```
@pytest.fixture
def some_fixture():
```

```
value = setup_value()
yield value
teardown_value(value)
```

By using `yield` instead of `return`, this is what happens:

- The fixture function is called
- It executes until the yield statement, where it pauses and yields the fixture value
- The test executes, receiving the fixture value as parameter
- Regardless of whether the test passes or fails, the function is resumed so it can perform its teardown actions

For those familiar with it, this is very similar to a **context manager** (https://docs.python.org/3/library/contextlib.html#contextlib.contextmanager), except that you don't need to surround the yield statement with a try/except clause to ensure the block after yield is executed, even if an exception occurs.

Let's return to our example; we can now use `yield` instead of `return` and close the file:

```
@pytest.fixture
def comedy_series():
    file = open("series.csv", "r", newline="")
    yield list(csv.reader(file))
    file.close()
```

This is good, but notice that because `yield` works well with the `with` statement of the file object, we can write this instead:

```
@pytest.fixture
def comedy_series():
    with open("series.csv", "r", newline="") as file:
        return list(csv.reader(file))
```

The file will be closed automatically by the `with` statement after the test completes, which is shorter and considered more Pythonic.

Awesome.

Composability

Suppose we receive a new series.csv file that now contains a much larger number of TV series, including the comedy series we had before and many other genres as well. We want to use this new data for some other tests, but we would like to keep existing tests working as they did previously.

Fixtures in pytest can easily depend on other fixtures just by declaring them as parameters. Using this property, we are able to create a new series fixture that reads all the data from `series.csv` (which now contains more genres), and change our `comedy_series` fixture to filter out only comedy series:

```
@pytest.fixture
def series():
    with open("series.csv", "r", newline="") as file:
        return list(csv.reader(file))

@pytest.fixture
def comedy_series(series):
    return [x for x in series if x[GENRE] == "comedy"]
```

The tests which use `comedy_series` are unchanged:

```
def test_highest_rated(comedy_series):
    assert highest_rated(comedy_series) == "Seinfeld"

def test_oldest(comedy_series):
    assert oldest(comedy_series) == "Seinfeld"
```

Note that, because of those characteristics, fixtures are a prime example of dependency injection, which is a technique where a function or an object declares its dependencies, but otherwise doesn't know or care how those dependencies will be created, or by who. This makes them extremely modular and reusable.

Sharing fixtures with conftest.py files

Suppose we need to use our `comedy_series` fixture from the previous section in other test modules. In pytest, sharing fixtures is easily done by just moving the fixture code to a `conftest.py` file.

A `conftest.py` file is a normal Python module, except that it is loaded automatically by pytest, and any fixtures defined in it are available to test modules in the same directory and below automatically. Consider this test module hierarchy:

```
tests/
    ratings/
        series.csv
        test_ranking.py
    io/
        conftest.py
        test_formats.py
```

```
conftest.py
```

The `tests/conftest.py` file is at the root of the hierarchy, so any fixtures defined on it are automatically available to all other test modules in this project. Fixtures in `tests/io/conftest.py` will be available only to modules at and below `tests/io`, so only to `test_formats.py` for now.

This might not look like a big deal, but it makes sharing fixtures a breeze: it is very liberating to be able to start small with just a few fixtures when writing a test module, knowing that if those fixtures are useful to other tests in the future, it will be just a small matter of moving the fixtures to a `conftest.py` to reuse them. This avoids the temptation to copy and paste test data around, or to spend too much time thinking about how to organize test-supporting code from the start, to avoid having to do a lot of refactoring later.

Scopes

Fixtures are always created when a test function requests them, by declaring them on the parameter list, as we've seen already. By default, each fixture is destroyed when each test finishes.

As mentioned at the beginning of this chapter, some fixtures can be costly to create or set up, and it would be helpful to be able to create as few instances of it as possible, to save time. Here are some examples:

- Initializing database tables
- Reading cached data from a disk, for example, large CSV data
- Starting up external services

To help solve this issue, fixtures in pytest can have different **scopes**. The scope of a fixture defines when the fixture should be cleaned up. While the fixture is not cleaned up, tests requesting the fixture will receive the same fixture value.

The scope parameter of the @pytest.fixture decorator is used to set the fixture's scope:

```
@pytest.fixture(scope="session")
def db_connection():
    ...
```

The following scopes are available:

- `scope="session"`: fixture is teardown when all tests finish.
- `scope="module"`: fixture is teardown when the last test function of a module finishes.
- `scope="class"`: fixture is teardown when the last test method of a class finishes.
- `scope="function"`: fixture is teardown when the test function requesting it finishes. This is the default.

It is important to emphasize that, regardless of scope, each fixture will be created only when a test function requires it. For example, session-scoped fixtures are not necessarily created at the start of the session, but only when the first test that requests it is about to be called. This makes sense when you consider that not all tests might need a session-scoped fixture, and there are various forms to run only a subset of tests, as we have seen in previous chapters.

Scopes in action

To show scopes in action, let's take a look at a common pattern that's used when your tests involve some form of database. In the upcoming example, don't focus on the database API (which is made up anyway), but on the concepts and design of the fixtures involved.

Usually, the connection to a database and table creation are slow. If the database supports transactions, which is the ability to perform a set of changes that can be applied or discarded atomically, then the following pattern can be used.

For starters, we can use a session-scoped fixture to connect and initialize the database with the tables we need:

```
@pytest.fixture(scope="session")
def db():
    db = connect_to_db("localhost", "test")
    db.create_table(Series)
    db.create_table(Actors)
    yield db
    db.prune()
    db.disconnect()
```

Note that we prune the test database and disconnect from it at the end of the fixture, which will happen at the end of the session.

With the db fixture, we can share the same database across all our tests. This is great, because it saves time. But it also has the downside that now tests can change the database and affect other tests. To solve that problem, we create a transaction fixture that starts a new transaction before a test starts and rolls the transaction back when the test finishes, ensuring the database returns to its previous state:

```
@pytest.fixture(scope="function")
def transaction(db):
    transaction = db.start_transaction()
    yield transaction
    transaction.rollback()
```

Note that our transaction fixture depends on db. Tests now can use the transaction fixture to read and write to the database at will, without worrying about cleaning it up for other tests:

```
def test_insert(transaction):
    transaction.add(Series("The Office", 2005, 8.8))
    assert transaction.find(name="The Office") is not None
```

With just these two fixtures, we have a very solid foundation to write our database tests with: the first test that requires the transaction fixture will automatically initialize the database through the db fixture, and each test from now on that needs to perform transactions will do so from a pristine database.

This composability between fixtures of different scopes is very powerful and enables all sorts of clever designs in real-world test suites.

Autouse

It is possible to apply a fixture to all of the tests in a hierarchy, even if the tests don't explicitly request a fixture, by passing autouse=True to the @pytest.fixture decorator. This is useful when we need to apply a side-effect before and/or after each test unconditionally.

```
@pytest.fixture(autouse=True)
def setup_dev_environment():
    previous = os.environ.get('APP_ENV', '')
    os.environ['APP_ENV'] = 'TESTING'
    yield
    os.environ['APP_ENV'] = previous
```

An autouse fixture is applied to all tests which the fixture is available for use with:

- Same module as the fixture
- Same class as the fixture, in the case of a fixture defined by a method
- Tests in the same directory or below, if the fixture is defined in a `conftest.py` file

In other words, if a test can access an autouse fixture by declaring it in the parameter list, the autouse fixture will be automatically used by that test. Note that it is possible for a test function to add the autouse fixture to its parameter list if it is interested in the return value of the fixture, as normal.

@pytest.mark.usefixtures

The `@pytest.mark.usefixtures` mark can be used to apply one or more fixtures to tests, as if they have the fixture name declared in their parameter list. This can be an alternative in situations where you want all tests in a group to always use a fixture that is not `autouse`.

For example, the code below will ensure all tests methods in the `TestVirtualEnv` class execute in a brand new virtual environment:

```
@pytest.fixture
def venv_dir():
    import venv

    with tempfile.TemporaryDirectory() as d:
        venv.create(d)
        pwd = os.getcwd()
        os.chdir(d)
        yield d
        os.chdir(pwd)

@pytest.mark.usefixtures('venv_dir')
class TestVirtualEnv:
    ...
```

As the name indicates, you can pass multiple fixtures names to the decorator:

```
@pytest.mark.usefixtures("venv_dir", "config_python_debug")
class Test:
    ...
```

Parametrizing fixtures

Fixtures can also be parametrized directly. When a fixture is parametrized, all tests that use the fixture will now run multiple times, once for each parameter. This is an excellent tool to use when we have variants of a fixture and each test that uses the fixture should also run with all variants.

In the previous chapter, we saw an example of parametrization using multiple implementations of a serializer:

```python
@pytest.mark.parametrize(
    "serializer_class",
    [JSONSerializer, XMLSerializer, YAMLSerializer],
)
class Test:

    def test_quantity(self, serializer_class):
        serializer = serializer_class()
        quantity = Quantity(10, "m")
        data = serializer.serialize_quantity(quantity)
        new_quantity = serializer.deserialize_quantity(data)
        assert new_quantity == quantity

    def test_pipe(self, serializer_class):
        serializer = serializer_class()
        pipe = Pipe(
            length=Quantity(1000, "m"), diameter=Quantity(35, "cm")
        )
        data = serializer.serialize_pipe(pipe)
        new_pipe = serializer.deserialize_pipe(data)
        assert new_pipe == pipe
```

We can update the example to parametrize on a fixture instead:

```python
class Test:

    @pytest.fixture(params=[JSONSerializer, XMLSerializer,
                            YAMLSerializer])
    def serializer(self, request):
        return request.param()

    def test_quantity(self, serializer):
        quantity = Quantity(10, "m")
        data = serializer.serialize_quantity(quantity)
        new_quantity = serializer.deserialize_quantity(data)
        assert new_quantity == quantity
```

```
def test_pipe(self, serializer):
    pipe = Pipe(
        length=Quantity(1000, "m"), diameter=Quantity(35, "cm")
    )
    data = serializer.serialize_pipe(pipe)
    new_pipe = serializer.deserialize_pipe(data)
    assert new_pipe == pipe
```

Note the following:

- We pass a `params` parameter to the fixture definition.
- We access the parameter inside the fixture, using the `param` attribute of the special `request` object. This built-in fixture provides access to the requesting test function and the parameter when the fixture is parametrized. We will see more about the `request` fixture later in this chapter.
- In this case, we instantiate the serializer inside the fixture, instead of explicitly in each test.

As can be seen, parametrizing a fixture is very similar to parametrizing a test, but there is one key difference: by parametrizing a fixture we make all tests that use that fixture run against all the parametrized instances, making them an excellent solution for fixtures shared in `conftest.py` files.

It is very rewarding to see a lot of new tests being automatically executed when you add a new parameter to an existing fixture.

Using marks from fixtures

We can use the `request` fixture to access marks that are applied to test functions.

Suppose we have an `autouse` fixture that always initializes the current locale to English:

```
@pytest.fixture(autouse=True)
def setup_locale():
    locale.setlocale(locale.LC_ALL, "en_US")
    yield
    locale.setlocale(locale.LC_ALL, None)

def test_currency_us():
    assert locale.currency(10.5) == "$10.50"
```

But what if we want to use a different locale for just a few tests?

One way to do that is to use a custom mark, and access the `mark` object from within our fixture:

```python
@pytest.fixture(autouse=True)
def setup_locale(request):
    mark = request.node.get_closest_marker("change_locale")
    loc = mark.args[0] if mark is not None else "en_US"
    locale.setlocale(locale.LC_ALL, loc)
    yield
    locale.setlocale(locale.LC_ALL, None)

@pytest.mark.change_locale("pt_BR")
def test_currency_br():
    assert locale.currency(10.5) == "R$ 10,50"
```

Marks can be used that way to pass information to fixtures. Because it is somewhat implicit though, I recommend using it sparingly, because it might lead to hard-to-understand code.

An overview of built-in fixtures

Let's take a look at some built-in pytest fixtures.

tmpdir

The `tmpdir` fixture provides an empty directory that is removed automatically at the end of each test:

```python
def test_empty(tmpdir):
    assert os.path.isdir(tmpdir)
    assert os.listdir(tmpdir) == []
```

Being a `function`-scoped fixture, each test gets its own directory so they don't have to worry about clean up or generating unique directories.

The fixture provides a `py.local` object (`http://py.readthedocs.io/en/latest/path.html`), from the `py` library (`http://py.readthedocs.io`), which provides convenient methods to deal with file paths, such as joining, reading, writing, getting the extension, and so on; it is similar in philosophy to the `pathlib.Path` object (`https://docs.python.org/3/library/pathlib.html`) from the standard library:

```python
def test_save_curves(tmpdir):
    data = dict(status_code=200, values=[225, 300])
    fn = tmpdir.join('somefile.json')
```

```
write_json(fn, data)
assert fn.read() == '{"status_code": 200, "values": [225, 300]}'
```

 Why pytest use py.local instead of pathlib.Path?
Pytest had been around for years before pathlib.Path came along and was incorporated into the standard library, and the py library was one the best solutions for path-like objects at the time. Core pytest developers are looking into how to adapt pytest to the now-standard pathlib.Path API.

tmpdir_factory

The tmpdir fixture is very handy, but it is only function-scoped: this has the downside that it can only be used by other function-scoped fixtures.

The tmpdir_factory fixture is a *session-scoped* fixture that allows creating empty and unique directories at any scope. This can be useful when we need to store data on to a disk in fixtures of other scopes, for example a session-scoped cache or a database file.

To show it in action, the images_dir fixture shown next uses tmpdir_factory to create a unique directory for the entire test session containing a series of sample image files:

```
@pytest.fixture(scope='session')
def images_dir(tmpdir_factory):
    directory = tmpdir_factory.mktemp('images')
    download_images('https://example.com/samples.zip', directory)
    extract_images(directory / 'samples.zip')
    return directory
```

Because this will be executed only once per session, it will save us considerable time when running the tests.

Tests can then use the images_dir fixture tests to easily access the sample image files:

```
def test_blur_filter(images_dir):
    output_image = apply_blur_filter(images_dir / 'rock1.png')
    ...
```

Keep in mind however that a directory created by this fixture is shared and will only be deleted at the end of the test session. This means that tests should not modify the contents of the directory; otherwise, they risk affecting other tests.

monkeypatch

In some situations, tests need features that are complex or hard to set up in a testing environment, for example:

- Clients to an external resource (for example GitHub's API), where access during testing might be impractical or too expensive
- Forcing a piece of code to behave as if on another platform, such as error handling
- Complex conditions or environments that are hard to reproduce locally or in the CI

The monkeypatch fixture allows you to cleanly overwrite functions, objects, and dictionary entries of the system being tested with other objects and functions, undoing all changes during test teardown. For example:

```
import getpass

def user_login(name):
    password = getpass.getpass()
    check_credentials(name, password)
    ...
```

In this code, user_login uses the getpass.getpass() function (https://docs.python.org/3/library/getpass.html) from the standard library to prompt for the user's password in the most secure manner available in the system. It is hard to simulate the actual entering of the password during testing because getpass tries to read directly from the terminal (as opposed to from sys.stdin) when possible.

We can use the monkeypatch fixture to bypass the call to getpass in the tests, transparently and without changing the application code:

```
def test_login_success(monkeypatch):
    monkeypatch.setattr(getpass, "getpass", lambda: "valid-pass")
    assert user_login("test-user")

def test_login_wrong_password(monkeypatch):
    monkeypatch.setattr(getpass, "getpass", lambda: "wrong-pass")
    with pytest.raises(AuthenticationError, match="wrong password"):
        user_login("test-user")
```

In the tests, we use `monkeypatch.setattr` to replace the real `getpass()` function of the `getpass` module with a dummy `lambda`, which returns a hard-coded password. In `test_login_success`, we return a known, good password to ensure the user can authenticate successfully, while in `test_login_wrong_password`, we use a bad password to ensure the authentication error is handled correctly. As mentioned before, the original `getpass()` function is restored automatically at the end of the test, ensuring we don't leak that change to other tests in the system.

How and where to patch

The `monkeypatch` fixture works by replacing an attribute of an object by another object (often called a *mock*), restoring the original object at the end of the test. A common problem when using this fixture is patching the wrong object, which causes the original function/object to be called instead of the mock one.

To understand the problem, we need to understand how `import` and `import from` work in Python.

Consider a module called `services.py`:

```
import subprocess

def start_service(service_name):
    subprocess.run(f"docker run {service_name}")
```

In this code, we are importing the `subprocess` module and bringing the `subprocess` module object into the `services.py` namespace. That's why we call `subprocess.run`: we are accessing the `run` function of the `subprocess` object in the `services.py` namespace.

Now consider the previous code written slightly differently:

```
from subprocess import run

def start_service(service_name):
    run(f"docker run {service_name}")
```

Here, we are importing the `subprocess` module but bringing the `run` function object into the `service.py` namespace. That's why `run` can be called directly in `start_service`, and the `subprocess` name is not even available (if you try to call `subprocess.run`, you will get a `NameError` exception).

We need to be aware of this difference, to properly `monkeypatch` the usage of `subprocess.run` in `services.py`.

In the first case, we need to replace the run function of the subprocess module, because that's how start_service uses it:

```
import subprocess
import services

def test_start_service(monkeypatch):
    commands = []
    monkeypatch.setattr(subprocess, "run", commands.append)
    services.start_service("web")
    assert commands == ["docker run web"]
```

In this code, both services.py and test_services.py have the reference to the same subprocess module object.

In the second case, however, services.py has a reference to the original run function in its own namespace. For this reason, the correct approach for the second case is to replace the run function in services.py 's namespace:

```
import services

def test_start_service(monkeypatch):
    commands = []
    monkeypatch.setattr(services, "run", commands.append)
    services.start_service("web")
    assert commands == ["docker run web"]
```

How the code being tested imports code that needs to be monkeypatched is the reason why people are tripped by this so often, so make sure you take a look at the code first.

capsys/capfd

The capsys fixture captures all text written to sys.stdout and sys.stderr and makes it available during testing.

Suppose we have a small command-line script and want to check the usage instructions are correct when the script is invoked without arguments:

```
from textwrap import dedent

def script_main(args):
    if not args:
        show_usage()
        return 0
    ...
```

```
def show_usage():
    print("Create/update webhooks.")
    print(" Usage: hooks REPO URL")
```

During testing, we can access the captured output, using the `capsys` fixture. This fixture has a `capsys.readouterr()` method that returns a `namedtuple` (https://docs.python.org/3/library/collections.html#collections.namedtuple) with `out` and `err` attributes, containing the captured text from `sys.stdout` and `sys.stderr` respectively:

```
def test_usage(capsys):
    script_main([])
    captured = capsys.readouterr()
    assert captured.out == dedent("""\
        Create/update webhooks.
          Usage: hooks REPO URL
    """)
```

There's also the `capfd` fixture that works similarly to `capsys`, except that it also captures the output of file descriptors `1` and `2`. This makes it possible to capture the standard output and standard errors, even for extension modules.

Binary mode

`capsysbinary` and `capfdbinary` are fixtures identical to `capsys` and `capfd`, except that they capture output in binary mode, and their `readouterr()` methods return raw bytes instead of text. It might be useful in specialized situations, for example, when running an external process that produces binary output, such as `tar`.

request

The `request` fixture is an internal pytest fixture that provides useful information about the requesting test. It can be declared in test functions and fixtures, and provides attributes such as the following:

- `function`: the Python `test` function object, available for `function`-scoped fixtures.
- `cls/instance`: the Python class/instance of a `test` method object, available for function- and `class`-scoped fixtures. It can be `None` if the fixture is being requested from a `test` function, as opposed to a test method.
- `module`: the Python module object of the requesting test method, available for `module`-, `function`-, and `class`-scoped fixtures.

- `session`: pytest's internal `Session` object, which is a singleton for the test session and represents the root of the collection tree. It is available to fixtures of all scopes.
- `node`: the pytest collection node, which wraps one of the Python objects discussed that matches the fixture scope.
- `addfinalizer(func)`: adds a new `finalizer` function that will be called at the end of the test. The finalizer function is called without arguments. `addfinalizer` was the original way to execute teardown in fixtures, but has since then been superseded by the `yield` statement, remaining in use mostly for backward compatibility.

Fixtures can use those attributes to customize their own behavior based on the test being executed. For example, we can create a fixture that provides a temporary directory using the current test name as the prefix of the temporary directory, somewhat similar to the built-in `tmpdir` fixture:

```
@pytest.fixture
def tmp_path(request) -> Path:
    with TemporaryDirectory(prefix=request.node.name) as d:
        yield Path(d)

def test_tmp_path(tmp_path):
    assert list(tmp_path.iterdir()) == []
```

This code created the following directory when executed on my system:

```
C:\Users\Bruno\AppData\Local\Temp\test_tmp_patht5w0cvd0
```

The `request` fixture can be used whenever you want to customize a fixture based on the attributes of the test being executed, or to access the marks applied to the test function, as we have seen in the previous sections.

Tips/discussion

The following are some short topics and tips that did not fit into the previous sections, but that I think are worth mentioning.

When to use fixtures, as opposed to simple functions

Sometimes, all you need is to construct a simple object for your tests, and arguably this can be done in a plain function, not necessarily needing to be implemented as a fixture. Suppose we have a `WindowManager` class, that does not receive any parameters:

```
class WindowManager:
    ...
```

One way to use it in our tests would be to write a fixture:

```
@pytest.fixture
def manager():
    return WindowManager()

def test_windows_creation(manager):
    window = manager.new_help_window("pipes_help.rst")
    assert window.title() == "Pipe Setup Help"
```

Alternatively, you could argue that a fixture for such simple usage is overkill, and use a plain function instead:

```
def create_window_manager():
    return WindowManager()

def test_windows_creation():
    manager = create_window_manager()
    window = manager.new_help_window("pipes_help.rst")
    assert window.title() == "Pipe Setup Help"
```

Or you could even create the manager explicitly on each test:

```
def test_windows_creation():
    manager = WindowManager()
    window = manager.new_help_window("pipes_help.rst")
    assert window.title() == "Pipe Setup Help"
```

This is perfectly fine, especially if this is used in a few tests in a single module.

Keep in mind, however, that fixtures **abstract away details about the construction and teardown process of objects**. This is crucial to remember when deciding to forego fixtures in favor of normal functions.

Suppose that our `WindowManager` now needs to be closed explicitly, or that it needs a local directory for logging purposes:

```
class WindowManager:

    def __init__(self, logging_directory):
        ...

    def close(self):
        """
        Close the WindowManager and all associated resources.
        """
        ...
```

If we have been using a fixture such as the one given in the first example, we just update the fixture function and **no tests need to change at all**:

```
@pytest.fixture
def manager(tmpdir):
    wm = WindowManager(str(tmpdir))
    yield wm
    wm.close()
```

But if we opted to use a plain function, now we **have to update all places that call our function**: we need to pass a logging directory and guarantee that `.close()` is called at the end of the test:

```
def create_window_manager(tmpdir, request):
    wm = WindowManager(str(tmpdir))
    request.addfinalizer(wm.close)
    return wm

def test_windows_creation(tmpdir, request):
    manager = create_window_manager(tmpdir, request)
    window = manager.new_help_window("pipes_help.rst")
    assert window.title() == "Pipe Setup Help"
```

Depending on how many times this function has been used in our tests, this can be quite a refactoring.

The message is: it is fine to use plain functions when the underlying object is simple and unlikely to change, but keep in mind that fixtures abstract the details of the creation/destruction of objects, and they might need to change in the future. On the other hand, using fixtures creates another level of indirection, which slightly increases code complexity. In the end, it is a balance that should be weighted by you.

Renaming fixtures

The `@pytest.fixture` decorator accepts a `name` parameter that can be used to specify a name for the fixture, different from the fixture function:

```
@pytest.fixture(name="venv_dir")
def _venv_dir():
    ...
```

This is useful, because there are some annoyances that might affect users when using fixtures declared in the same module as the test functions that use them:

- If users forget to declare the fixture in the parameter list of a test function, they will get a `NameError` instead of the fixture function object (because they are in the same module).
- Some linters complain that the test function parameter is shadowing the fixture function.

You might adopt this as a good practice in your team if the previous annoyances are frequent. Keep in mind that these problems only happen with fixtures defined in test modules, not in `conftest.py` files.

Prefer local imports in conftest files

`conftest.py` files are imported during collection, so they directly affect your experience when running tests from the command line. For this reason, I suggest using local imports in `conftest.py` files as often as possible, to keep import times low.

So, don't use this:

```
import pytest
import tempfile
from myapp import setup

@pytest.fixture
def setup_app():
    ...
```

Prefer local imports:

```
import pytest

@pytest.fixture
def setup_app():
    import tempfile
    from myapp import setup
    ...
```

This practice has a noticeable impact on test startup in large test suites.

Fixtures as test-supporting code

You should think of fixtures not only as a means of providing resources, but also of providing supporting code for your tests. By supporting code, I mean classes that provide high-level functionality for testing.

For example, a bot framework might provide a fixture that can be used to test your bot as a black box:

```
def test_hello(bot):
    reply = bot.say("hello")
    assert reply.text == "Hey, how can I help you?"

def test_store_deploy_token(bot):
    assert bot.store["TEST"]["token"] is None
    reply = bot.say("my token is ASLKM8KJAN")
    assert reply.text == "OK, your token was saved"
    assert bot.store["TEST"]["token"] == "ASLKM8KJAN"
```

The bot fixture allows the developer to talk to the bot, verify responses, and check the contents of the internal store that is handled by the framework, among other things. It provides a high-level interface that makes tests easier to write and understand, even for those who do not understand the internals of the framework.

This technique is useful for applications, because it will make it easy and enjoyable for developers to add new tests. It is also useful for libraries, because they will provide high-level testing support for users of your library.

Summary

In this chapter, we delved into one of pytest's most famous features: fixtures. We have seen how they can be used to provide resources and test functionality, and how to concisely express setup/teardown code. We learned how to share fixtures, using `conftest.py` files; to use fixture scopes, to avoid creating expensive resources for every test; and to autouse fixtures that are executed for all tests in the same module or hierarchy. Then, we learned how to parametrize fixtures and use marks from them. We took an overview of various built-in fixtures, and closed the chapter with some short discussions about fixtures in general. I hope you enjoyed the ride!

In the next chapter, we will explore a little of the vast pytest plugin ecosystem that is at your disposal.

5
Plugins

In the previous chapter, we explored one of the most important features of pytest: fixtures. We learned how we can use fixtures to manage resources and make our lives easier when writing tests.

pytest is constructed with customization and flexibility in mind, and allows developers to write powerful extensions called **plugins**. Plugins in pytest can do all sorts of things, from simply providing a new fixture, all the way to adding command line options, changing how tests are executed, and even running tests written in other languages.

In this chapter, we will do the following:

- Learn how to find and install plugins
- Have a taste of what plugins the ecosystem has to offer

Finding and installing plugins

As mentioned at the beginning of the chapter, pytest is written from the ground up with customization and flexibility in mind. The plugin mechanism is at the core of the pytest architecture, so much so that many of pytest's built-in features are implemented in terms of internal plugins, such as marks, parametrization, fixtures—nearly everything, even command-line options.

This flexibility has led to an enormous and rich plugin ecosystem. At the time of writing, the number of plugins available is over 500, and that number keeps increasing at an astonishing rate.

Finding plugins

Given the large number of plugins, it would be nice if there was a site that showed all pytest plugins along with their descriptions. It would also be nice if this place also showed information about compatibility with different Python and pytest versions.

Well, the good news is that such a site exists, and it is maintained by the core development team: pytest plugin compatibility (`http://plugincompat.herokuapp.com/`). On it, you will find a list of all the pytest plugins available in PyPI, along with Python- and pytest-version compatibility information. The site is fed daily with new plugins and updates directly from PyPI, making it a great place to browse for new plugins.

Installing plugins

Plugins are usually installed with `pip`:

```
λ pip install <PLUGIN_NAME>
```

For example, to install `pytest-mock`, we execute the following:

```
λ pip install pytest-mock
```

No registration of any kind is necessary; pytest automatically detects the installed plugins in your virtual environment or Python installation.

This simplicity makes it dead easy to try out new plugins.

An overview of assorted plugins

Now, we will take a look at some useful and/or interesting plugins. Of course, it is not possible to cover all plugins here, so we will try to cover the ones that cover popular frameworks and general capabilities, with a few obscure plugins thrown in. Of course, this barely scratches the surface, but let's get to it.

pytest-xdist

This is a very popular plugin and is maintained by the core developers; it allows you to run tests under multiple CPUs, to speed up the test run.

After installing it, simply use the -n command-line flag to use the given number of CPUs to run the tests:

```
λ pytest -n 4
```

And that's it! Now, your tests will run across four cores and hopefully speed up the test suite quite a bit, if it is CPU intensive, thought I/O-bound tests won't see much improvement, though. You can also use -n auto to let pytest-xdist automatically figure out the number of CPUs you have available.

 Keep in mind that when your tests are running concurrently, and in random order, they must be careful to avoid stepping on each other's toes, for example, reading/writing to the same directory. While they should be idempotent anyway, running the tests in a random order often brings attention to problems that were lying dormant until then.

pytest-cov

The pytest-cov plugin provides integration with the popular coverage module, which provides detailed coverage reports for your code when running tests. This lets you detect sections of code that are not covered by any test code, which is an opportunity to write more tests to cover those cases.

After installation, you can use the --cov option to provide a coverage report at the end of the test run:

```
λ pytest --cov=src
...
----------- coverage: platform win32, python 3.6.3-final-0 -----------
Name                      Stmts   Miss   Cover
----------------------------------------------
src/series.py               108      5    96%
src/tests/test_series        22      0   100%
----------------------------------------------
TOTAL                       130      5    97%
```

The --cov option accepts a path to source files that should have reports generated, so you should pass your src or package directory depending on your project's layout.

You can also use the --cov-report option to generate reports in various formats: XML, annotate, and HTML. The latter is especially useful to use locally because it generates HTML files showing your code, with missed lines highlighted in red, making it very easy to find those uncovered spots.

This plugin also works with `pytest-xdist` out of the box.

Finally, the `.coverage` file generated by this plugin is compatible with many online services that provide coverage tracking and reporting, such as `coveralls.io` (`https://coveralls.io/`) and `codecov.io` (`https://codecov.io/`).

pytest-faulthandler

This plugin automatically enables the built-in `faulthandler` (`https://docs.python.org/3/library/faulthandler.html`) module when running your tests, which outputs Python tracebacks in catastrophic cases such as a segmentation fault. After installed, no other setup or flag is required; the `faulthandler` module will be enabled automatically.

This plugin is strongly recommended if you regularly use extension modules written in C/C++, as those are more susceptible to crashes.

pytest-mock

The `pytest-mock` plugin provides a fixture that allows a smoother integration between pytest and the `unittest.mock` (`https://docs.python.org/3/library/unittest.mock.html`) module of the standard library. It provides functionality similar to the built-in `monkeypatch` fixture, but the mock objects produced by `unittest.mock` also record information on how they are accessed. This makes many common testing tasks easier, such as verifying that a mocked function has been called, and with which arguments.

The plugin provides a `mocker` fixture that can be used for patching classes and methods. Using the `getpass` example from the last chapter, here is how you could write it using this plugin:

```
import getpass

def test_login_success(mocker):
    mocked = mocker.patch.object(getpass, "getpass",
                                 return_value="valid-pass")
    assert user_login("test-user")
    mocked.assert_called_with("enter password: ")
```

Note that besides replacing `getpass.getpass()` and always returning the same value, we can also ensure that the `getpass` function has been called with the correct arguments.

The same advice on how and where to patch the `monkeypatch` fixture from the previous chapter also applies when using this plugin.

pytest-django

As the name suggests, this plugin allows you to test your `Django` (`https://www.djangoproject.com/`) applications using pytest. `Django` is one of the most famous web frameworks in use today.

The plugin provides a ton of features:

- A very nice Quick Start tutorial
- Command-line and `pytest.ini` options to configure Django
- Compatibility with `pytest-xdist`
- Database access using the `django_db` mark, with automatic transaction rollback between tests, as well as a bunch of fixtures that let you control how the database is managed
- Fixtures to make requests to your application: `client`, `admin_client`, and `admin_user`
- A `live_server` fixture that runs a `Django` server in a background thread

All in all, this is one of the most complete plugins available in the ecosystem, with too many features to cover here. It is a must-have for `Django` applications, so make sure to check out its extensive documentation.

pytest-flakes

This plugin allows you to check your code using `pyflakes` (`https://pypi.org/project/pyflakes/`), which is a static checker of source files for common errors, such as missing imports and unknown variables.

After installed, use the `--flakes` option to activate it:

```
λ pytest pytest-flakes.py --flake
...
============================ FAILURES ============================
_____ pyflakes-check _____
```

```
CH5\pytest-flakes.py:1: UnusedImport
'os' imported but unused
CH5\pytest-flakes.py:6: UndefinedName
undefined name 'unknown'
```

This will run the flake checks alongside your normal tests, making it an easy and cheap way to keep your code tidy and prevent some errors. The plugin also keeps a local cache of files that have not changed since the last check, so it is fast and convenient to use locally.

pytest-asyncio

The asyncio (https://docs.python.org/3/library/asyncio.html) module is one of the hot new additions to Python 3, providing a new framework for asynchronous applications. The pytest-asyncio plugin lets you write asynchronous test functions, making it a snap to test your asynchronous code.

All you need to do is make your test function async def and mark it with the asyncio mark:

```
@pytest.mark.asyncio
async def test_fetch_requests():
    requests = await fetch_requests("example.com/api")
    assert len(requests) == 2
```

The plugin also manages the event loop behind the scenes, providing a few options on how to change it if you need to use a custom event loop.

> You are, of course, free to have normal synchronous test functions along with the asynchronous ones.

pytest-trio

Trio's motto is Pythonic async I/O for humans (https://trio.readthedocs.io/en/latest/). It uses the same async def/await keywords of the asyncio standard module, but it is considered simpler and more friendly to use, containing some novel ideas about how to deal with timeouts and groups of parallel tasks in a way to avoid common errors in parallel programming. It is definitely worth checking out if you are into asynchronous development.

pytest-trio works similarly to pytest-asyncio: you write asynchronous test functions and mark them using the trio mark. It also provides other functionality that makes testing easier and more reliable, such as controllable clocks for testing timeouts, special functions to deal with tasks, mocking network sockets and streams, and a lot more.

pytest-tornado

Tornado (http://www.tornadoweb.org/en/stable/) is a web framework and asynchronous network library. It is very mature, works in Python 2 and 3, and the standard asyncio module borrowed many ideas and concepts from it.

pytest-asyncio was heavily inspired by pytest-tornado, so it works with the same idea of using a gen_test to mark your test as a coroutine. It uses the yield keyword instead of await, as it supports Python 2, but otherwise it looks very similar:

```
@pytest.mark.gen_test
def test_tornado(http_client):
    url = "https://docs.pytest.org/en/latest"
    response = yield http_client.fetch(url)
    assert response.code == 200
```

pytest-postgresql

This plugin allows you to test code that needs a running PostgreSQL database.

Here's a quick example of it in action:

```
def test_fetch_series(postgresql):
    cur = postgresql.cursor()
    cur.execute('SELECT * FROM comedy_series;')
    assert len(cur.fetchall()) == 5
    cur.close()
```

It provides two fixtures:

- postgresql: a client fixture that starts and closes connections to the running test database. At the end of the test, it drops the test database to ensure tests don't interfere with one another.
- postgresql_proc: a session-scoped fixture that starts the PostgreSQL process once per session and ensures that it stops at the end.

It also provides several configuration options on how to connect and configure the testing database.

docker-services

This plugin starts and manages Docker services you need in order to test your code. This makes it simple to run the tests because you don't need to manually start the services yourself; the plugin will start and stop them during the test session, as needed.

You configure the services using a `.services.yaml` file; here is a simple example:

```
database:
    image: postgres
    environment:
        POSTGRES_USERNAME: pytest-user
        POSTGRES_PASSWORD: pytest-pass
        POSTGRES_DB: test
    image: regis:10
```

This will start two services: `postgres` and `redis`.

With that, all that's left to do is to run your suite with the following:

```
pytest --docker-services
```

The plugin takes care of the rest.

pytest-selenium

Selenium is a framework targeted to automating browsers, to test web applications (`https://www.seleniumhq.org/`). It lets you do things such as opening a web page, clicking on a button, and then ensuring that a certain page loads, all programmatically. It supports all the major browsers out there and has a thriving community.

`pytest-selenium` provides you with a fixture that lets you write tests that do all of those things, taking care of setting up `Selenium` for you.

Here's a basic example of how to visit a page, click on a link, and check the title of the loaded page:

```
def test_visit_pytest(selenium):
    selenium.get("https://docs.pytest.org/en/latest/")
    assert "helps you write better programs" in selenium.title
```

```
elem = selenium.find_element_by_link_text("Contents")
elem.click()
assert "Full pytest documentation" in selenium.title
```

`Selenium` and `pytest-selenium` are sophisticated enough to test a wide range of applications, from static pages to full single-page frontend applications.

pytest-html

`pytest-html` generates beautiful HTML reports of your test results. After installing the plugin, simply run this:

```
λ pytest --html=report.html
```

This will generate a `report.html` file at the end of the test session.

Because pictures speak louder than words, here is an example:

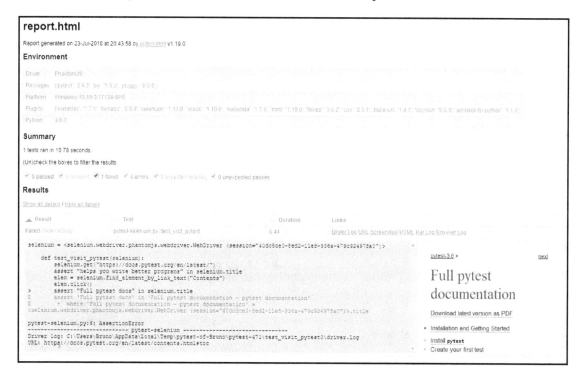

The reports can be served in a web server for easier viewing, plus they contain nice functionality such as checkboxes to show/hide different types of test results, and other plugins such as `pytest-selenium` are even able to attach screenshots to failed tests, as in the previous image.

It's definitely worth checking out.

pytest-cpp

To prove the point that pytest's framework is very flexible, the `pytest-cpp` plugin allows you to run tests written in Google Test (`https://github.com/google/googletest`) or Boost.Test (`https://www.boost.org`), which are frameworks for writing and running tests in the C++ language.

After they are installed, you just need to run pytest as normal:

```
λ pytest bin/tests
```

Pytest will find executable files containing test cases, detecting automatically whether they are written in `Google Test` or `Boost.Python`. It will run the tests and report results normally, with neat formatting that is familiar to pytest users.

Running those tests with pytest means that they now can make use of several features, such as parallel running with `pytest-xdist`, test selection with `-k`, JUnitXML reports, and so on. This plugin is particularly useful for code bases that use Python and C++ because it allows you to run all tests with a single command, and you can obtain a unique report.

pytest-timeout

The `pytest-timeout` plugin terminates tests automatically after they reach a certain timeout.

You use it by setting a global timeout in the command-line:

```
λ pytest --timeout=60
```

Or you can mark individual tests with the `@pytest.mark.timeout` mark:

```
@pytest.mark.timeout(600)
def test_long_simulation():
    ...
```

It works by using one of the two following methods to implement its timeout mechanism:

- `thread`: during test setup, the plugin starts a thread that sleeps for the desired timeout period. If the thread wakes up, it will dump the tracebacks of all the threads to `stderr` and kill the current process. If the test finishes before the thread wakes up, then the thread is cancelled and the test run continues. This is the method that works on all platforms.
- `signal`: a `SIGALRM` is scheduled during test setup and canceled when the test finishes. If the alarm is triggered, it will dump the tracebacks of all threads to `stderr` and fail the test, but it will allow the test run to continue. The advantage over the thread method is that it won't cancel the entire run when a timeout occurs, but it is not supported on all platforms.

The method is chosen automatically based on platform, but it can be changed in the command line or per-test by passing the `method=` parameter to `@pytest.mark.timeout`.

This plugin is indispensable in large test suites to avoid having tests hanging the CI.

pytest-annotate

Pyannotate (`https://github.com/dropbox/pyannotate`) is a project that observes runtime type information and can use that information to insert type annotations into the source code, and `pytest-annotate` makes it easy to use with pytest.

Let's get back to this simple test case:

```python
def highest_rated(series):
    return sorted(series, key=itemgetter(2))[-1][0]

def test_highest_rated():
    series = [
        ("The Office", 2005, 8.8),
        ("Scrubs", 2001, 8.4),
        ("IT Crowd", 2006, 8.5),
        ("Parks and Recreation", 2009, 8.6),
        ("Seinfeld", 1989, 8.9),
    ]
    assert highest_rated(series) == "Seinfeld"
```

After installing `pytest-annotate`, we can generate an annotations file passing the `--annotations-output` flag:

```
λ pytest --annotate-output=annotations.json
```

This will run the test suite as usual, but it will collect type information for later use.

Afterward, you can call `PyAnnotate` to apply the type information directly to the source code:

```
λ pyannotate --type-info annotations.json -w
Refactored test_series.py
--- test_series.py (original)
+++ test_series.py (refactored)
@@ -1,11 +1,15 @@
 from operator import itemgetter
+from typing import List
+from typing import Tuple


 def highest_rated(series):
+    # type: (List[Tuple[str, int, float]]) -> str
     return sorted(series, key=itemgetter(2))[-1][0]


 def test_highest_rated():
+    # type: () -> None
     series = [
         ("The Office", 2005, 8.8),
         ("Scrubs", 2001, 8.4),
Files that were modified:
pytest-annotate.py
```

It is very neat to quickly and efficiently annotate a large code base, especially if that code base is well covered by tests.

pytest-qt

The `pytest-qt` plugin allows you to write tests for GUI applications written in the Qt framework (https://www.qt.io/), supporting the more popular sets of Python bindings for Qt: `PyQt4`/`PyQt5`, and `PySide`/`PySide2`.

It provides a `qtbot` fixture that has methods to interact with a GUI application, such as clicking on buttons, entering text in fields, waiting for windows to pop up, and others. Here's a quick example showing it in action:

```
def test_main_window(qtbot):
    widget = MainWindow()
    qtbot.addWidget(widget)
    qtbot.mouseClick(widget.about_button, QtCore.Qt.LeftButton)
```

```
qtbot.waitUntil(widget.about_box.isVisible)
assert widget.about_box.text() == 'This is a GUI App'
```

Here, we create a window, click on the **about** button, wait for the **about** box to show up, and then ensure it shows the text we expect.

It also contains other goodies:

- Utilities to wait for specific Qt signals
- Automatic capturing of errors in virtual methods
- Automatic capturing of Qt logging messages

pytest-randomly

Tests ideally should be independent from each other, making sure to clean up after themselves so they can be run in any order and don't affect one another in any way.

pytest-randomly helps you keep your test suite true to that point, by randomly ordering tests, changing their order every time you run your test suite. This helps detect whether the tests have hidden inter-dependencies that you would not find otherwise.

It shuffles the order of the test items at module level, then at class level, and finally at the order of functions. It also resets random.seed() before each test to a fixed number, which is shown at the beginning of the test section. The random seed can be used at a later time to reproduce the same order with the --randomly-seed command line to reproduce a failure.

As an extra bonus, it also has special support for factory boy (https://factoryboy.readthedocs.io/en/latest/reference.html), faker (https://pypi.python.org/pypi/faker), and numpy (http://www.numpy.org/) libraries, resetting their random state before each test.

pytest-datadir

Often, tests need a supporting file, for example a CSV file containing data about comedy series, as we saw in the last chapter. pytest-datadir allows you to save files alongside your tests and easily access them from the tests in a safe manner.

Suppose you have a file structure such as this:

```
tests/
    test_series.py
```

In addition to this, you have a `series.csv` file that you need to access from tests defined in `test_series.py`.

With `pytest-datadir` installed, all you need to do is to create a directory with the name of the test file in the same directory and put the file there:

```
tests/
    test_series/
        series.csv
    test_series.py
```

The `test_series` directory and `series.csv` should be saved to your version-control system.

Now, tests in `test_series.py` can use the `datadir` fixture to access the file:

```python
def test_ratings(datadir):
    with open(datadir / "series.csv", "r", newline="") as f:
        data = list(csv.reader(f))
    ...
```

`datadir` is a Path instance pointing to the data directory (`https://docs.python.org/3/library/pathlib.html`).

One important thing to note is that when we use the `datadir` fixture in a test, we are not accessing the path to the original file, but a temporary copy. This ensures that tests can modify the files inside the data directory without affecting other tests because each test has its own copy.

pytest-regressions

It is normally the case that your application or library contains functionality that produces a data set as the result.

Testing these results is often tedious and error-prone, producing tests such as this:

```python
def test_obtain_series_asserts():
    data = obtain_series()
    assert data[0]["name"] == "The Office"
    assert data[0]["year"] == 2005
```

```
    assert data[0]["rating"] == 8.8
    assert data[1]["name"] == "Scrubs"
    assert data[1]["year"] == 2001
    ...
```

This gets old very quickly. Also, if any of the assertion fails, then the test stops at that point, and you won't know whether any other asserts after that point would also have failed. In other words, you don't get a clear picture of the overall failures. Most of all, this is also heavily unmaintainable because if the data returned by `obtain_series()` ever changes, you are in for a tedious and error-prone task of updating all the code.

`pytest-regressions` provides fixtures to solve this kind of problem. General data such as the previous example is a job for the `data_regression` fixture:

```
def test_obtain_series(data_regression):
    data = obtain_series()
    data_regression.check(data)
```

The first time you execute this test, it will fail with a message such as this:

```
...
E Failed: File not found in data directory, created:
E - CH5\test_series\test_obtain_series.yml
```

It will dump the data passed to `data_regression.check()` in a nicely formatted YAML file into the data directory of the `test_series.py` file (courtesy of the `pytest-datadir` fixture we saw earlier):

```
- name: The Office
  rating: 8.8
  year: 2005
- name: Scrubs
  rating: 8.4
  year: 2001
- name: IT Crowd
  rating: 8.5
  year: 2006
- name: Parks and Recreation
  rating: 8.6
  year: 2009
- name: Seinfeld
  rating: 8.9
  year: 1989
```

The next time you run this test, `data_regression` now compares the data passed to `data_regressions.check()` with the data found in `test_obtain_series.yml` inside the data directory. If they match, the test passes.

If the data is changed, however, the test fails with a nicely formatted text differential between the new data and the recorded one:

```
E AssertionError: FILES DIFFER:
E ---
E
E +++
E
E @@ -13,3 +13,6 @@
E
E  - name: Seinfeld
E    rating: 8.9
E    year: 1989
E +- name: Rock and Morty
E +  rating: 9.3
E +  year: 2013
```

In some cases, this might be a regression, in which case you can hunt down the bug in the code.

But in this case, the new data is *correct*; you just need to run pytest with the `--force-regen` flag and `pytest-regressions` will update the data file with the new content for you:

```
E Failed: Files differ and --force-regen set, regenerating file at:
E - CH5\test_series\test_obtain_series.yml
```

Now, the test passes if we run it again, as the file contains the new data.

This is an immense time saver when you have dozens of tests that suddenly produce different but correct results. You can bring them all up to date with a single pytest execution.

I use this plugin myself, and I can't count the hours it has saved me.

Honorable mentions

There are just too many good plugins to fit into this chapter. The previous sample is really just a small taste, where I tried to strike a balance between useful, interesting, and showing the flexibility of the plugin architecture.

Here are a few other plugins that are worth mentioning:

- `pytest-bdd`: a behavior-driven development for pytest
- `pytest-benchmark`: a fixture to benchmark code. It outputs benchmark results with color output
- `pytest-csv`: outputs test status as CSV files
- `pytest-docker-compose`: this manages Docker containers, using Docker compose during test runs
- `pytest-excel`: outputs test status reports in Excel
- `pytest-git`: provides a git fixture for tests that need to deal with git repositories
- `pytest-json`: outputs test statuses as json files
- `pytest-leaks`: detects memory leaks, by running tests repeatedly and comparing reference counts
- `pytest-menu`: lets the user select tests to run from a menu in the console
- `pytest-mongo`: process and client fixtures for MongoDB
- `pytest-mpl`: plugin that tests figures output from Matplotlib
- `pytest-mysql`: process and client fixtures for MySQL
- `pytest-poo`: replaces the F character for failing tests with the "pile of poo" emoji
- `pytest-rabbitmq`: process and client fixtures for RabbitMQ
- `pytest-redis`: process and client fixtures for Redis
- `pytest-repeat`: repeats all tests or specific tests a number of times to find intermittent failures
- `pytest-replay`: saves test runs and allows the user to execute them later, so as to reproduce crashes and flaky tests
- `pytest-rerunfailures`: this marks tests that can be run more than once to eliminate flaky tests
- `pytest-sugar`: changes the look and feel of the pytest console, by adding progress bars, emojis, instant failures, and so on
- `pytest-tap`: toutputs test reports in TAP format
- `pytest-travis-fold`: folds captured output and coverage reports in the Travis CI build log
- `pytest-vagrant`: pytest fixture that works with vagrant boxes
- `pytest-vcr`: automatically manages `VCR.py` cassettes (`https://vcrpy.readthedocs.io/en/latest/`), using a simple mark
- `pytest-virtualenv`: this provides a virtualenv fixture to manage virtual environments in tests

- `pytest-watch`: this continuously watches for changes in the source code and reruns pytest
- `pytest-xvfb`: this runs `Xvfb` (a virtual frame buffer) for your UI tests
- `tavern`: is tan automated test for APIs using a YAML-based syntax
- `xdoctest`: rewrite of the built-in doctests module, to make doctests easier to write and simpler to configure

Remember, at the time of writing, the number of pytest plugins available is over 500, so make sure to browse the list of plugins so that you can find something to your liking.

Summary

In this chapter, we looked at how easy it is to find and install plugins. We also have been shown some plugins that I use daily and find interesting. I hope this has given you a taste of what's possible in pytest, but please explore the vast number of plugins to see whether you can find any that are useful.

Creating your own plugins is not a topic that is covered in this book, but if you are interested, here are some resources to get you started:

- The pytest documentation: writing plugins (`https://docs.pytest.org/en/latest/writing_plugins.html`).
- Brian Okken's wonderful book about pytest Python testing with pytest, which delves deeper than this book does, has an excellent chapter on how to write your own plugins.

In the next chapter, we will learn how to use pytest with existing `unittest`-based test suites, including tips and suggestions on how to migrate them and incrementally use more of pytest's features.

6
Converting unittest suites to pytest

In the previous chapter, we have seen how the flexible pytest architecture has created a rich plugin ecosystem, with hundreds of plugins available. We learned how easy it is to find and install plugins, and had an overview of a number of interesting plugins.

Now that you are proficient with pytest, you might be in a situation where you have one or more `unittest`-based test suites and want to start using pytest with them. In this chapter, we will discuss the best approaches to start doing just that, ranging from simple test suites that might require little to no modification, to large in-house-grown test suites that contain all kinds of customizations grown organically over the years. Most of the tips and advice in this chapter come from my own experience when migrating our massive `unittest`-style test suite at ESSS (`https://wwww.esss.co`), where I work.

Here is what we will cover in this chapter:

- Using pytest as a test runner
- Converting asserts with `unittest2pytest`
- Handling setup and teardown
- Managing test hierarchies
- Refactoring test utilities
- Migration strategy

Using pytest as a test runner

One thing that surprisingly many people don't know is that pytest can run `unittest` suites out of the box, without any modifications.

For example:

```
class Test(unittest.TestCase):

    @classmethod
    def setUpClass(cls):
        cls.temp_dir = Path(tempfile.mkdtemp())
        cls.filepath = cls.temp_dir / "data.csv"
        cls.filepath.write_text(DATA.strip())

    @classmethod
    def tearDownClass(cls):
        shutil.rmtree(cls.temp_dir)

    def setUp(self):
        self.grids = list(iter_grids_from_csv(self.filepath))

    def test_read_properties(self):
        self.assertEqual(self.grids[0], GridData("Main Grid", 48, 44))
        self.assertEqual(self.grids[1], GridData("2nd Grid", 24, 21))
        self.assertEqual(self.grids[2], GridData("3rd Grid", 24, 48))

    def test_invalid_path(self):
        with self.assertRaises(IOError):
            list(iter_grids_from_csv(Path("invalid file")))

    @unittest.expectedFailure
    def test_write_properties(self):
        self.fail("not implemented yet")
```

We can run this using the `unittest` runner:

```
..x
--------------------- -------------------------------------------------
Ran 3 tests in 0.005s

OK (expected failures=1)
```

But the cool thing is that pytest also runs this test without any modifications:

```
λ pytest test_simple.py
========================= test session starts =========================
...
collected 3 items

test_simple.py ..x                                             [100%]

================= 2 passed, 1 xfailed in 0.11 seconds =================
```

This makes it really easy to just start using pytest as a test runner, which brings several benefits:

- You can use plugins—for example, `pytest-xdist`, to speed up the test suite.
- You have several command-line options at your disposal: `-k` for selecting tests, `--pdb` to jump into the debugger on errors, `--lf` to run last failed tests only, and so on.
- You can stop writing `self.assert*` methods and go with plain `assert`s. pytest will happily provide rich failure information, even for `unittest`-based subclasses.

For completeness, here are the `unittest` idioms and features supported out of the box:

- `setUp` and `tearDown` for function-level `setup/teardown`
- `setUpClass` and `tearDownClass` for class-level `setup/teardown`
- `setUpModule` and `tearDownModule` for module-level `setup/teardown`
- `skip`, `skipIf`, `skipUnless`, and `expectedFailure` decorators, for functions and classes
- `TestCase.skipTest` to imperatively skip inside tests

The following idioms are currently not supported:

- `load_tests protocol`: This protocol allows users to completely customize which tests are loaded from a module (`https://docs.python.org/3/library/unittest.html#load-tests-protocol`). The collection concept used by pytest is not compatible with how `load_tests` protocol works, so no work is planned by the pytest core team to support this feature (see the `#992` (`https://github.com/pytest-dev/pytest/issues/992`) issue if you are interested in the details).
- `subtests`: Tests using this feature can report multiple failures inside the same test method (`https://docs.python.org/3/library/unittest.html#distinguishing-test-iterations-using-subtests`). This feature is similar to pytest's own parametrization support, with the difference that the test results can be determined at runtime instead of collection time. In theory, this can be supported by pytest, and the feature is currently being tracked by issue `#1367` (`https://github.com/pytest-dev/pytest/issues/1367`).

Surprises with `pytest-xdist`
If you decide to use `pytest-xdist` in your test suite, be aware that it runs tests in an arbitrary order: each worker will run tests as they finish other tests, so the order the in which the tests are executed is not predictable. Because the default `unittest` runner runs tests sequentially and always in the same order, often this will bring to light concurrency problems to your test suite—for example, tests trying to create a temporary directory with the same name. You should see this as an opportunity to fix the underlying concurrency problems, as they should not be part of the test suite anyway.

Pytest features in unittest subclasses

Although not designed to support all its features when running `unittest`-based tests, a few of the pytest idioms are supported:

- **Plain asserts**: pytest assertion introspect works just as well when subclassing `unittest.TestCase`
- **Marks**: marks can be applied normally to `unittest` test methods and classes. Plugins that deal with marks should work normally in most cases (for example, `pytest-timeout` marks)
- **Autouse** fixtures: autouse fixtures defined in modules or `conftest.py` files will be created/destroyed when executing `unittest` test methods normally, including `unittest` subclasses in the case of class-scoped autouse fixtures
- **Test selection**: `-k` and `-m` in the command line should work as normal

Other pytest features do not work with `unittest`, especially:

- **Fixtures**: `unittest` test methods cannot request fixtures. Pytest uses `unittest`'s own result collector to execute the tests, which doesn't support passing arguments to test functions
- **Parametrization**: this is not supported, for similar reasons as for fixtures: we need to pass the parametrized values, and this is not currently possible

Plugins that don't rely on fixtures may work normally, for example `pytest-timeout` or `pytest-randomly`.

Converting asserts with unitest2pytest

Once you have changed the test runner to pytest, you can take advantage of writing plain assert statements instead of `self.assert*` methods.

Converting all the method calls is boring and error-prone, that's why the `unittest2pytest` tool exists. It converts all `self.assert*` method calls to plain asserts, and also converts `self.assertRaises` calls to the appropriate pytest idiom.

Install it using `pip`:

```
λ pip install unittest2pytest
```

Once installed, you can now execute it on the files you want:

```
λ unittest2pytest test_simple2.py
RefactoringTool: Refactored test_simple2.py
--- test_simple2.py (original)
+++ test_simple2.py (refactored)
@@ -5,6 +5,7 @@
 import unittest
 from collections import namedtuple
 from pathlib import Path
+import pytest

 DATA = """
 Main Grid,48,44
@@ -49,12 +50,12 @@
         self.grids = list(iter_grids_from_csv(self.filepath))

     def test_read_properties(self):
-        self.assertEqual(self.grids[0], GridData("Main Grid", 48, 44))
-        self.assertEqual(self.grids[1], GridData("2nd Grid", 24, 21))
-        self.assertEqual(self.grids[2], GridData("3rd Grid", 24, 48))
+        assert self.grids[0] == GridData("Main Grid", 48, 44)
+        assert self.grids[1] == GridData("2nd Grid", 24, 21)
+        assert self.grids[2] == GridData("3rd Grid", 24, 48)

     def test_invalid_path(self):
-        with self.assertRaises(IOError):
+        with pytest.raises(IOError):
             list(iter_grids_from_csv(Path("invalid file")))

     @unittest.expectedFailure
RefactoringTool: Files that need to be modified:
RefactoringTool: test_simple2.py
```

By default, it won't touch the files and will only show the difference in the changes it could apply. To actually apply the changes, pass `-wn` (`--write` and `--nobackups`).

Note that in the previous example, it correctly replaced the `self.assert*` calls, `self.assertRaises`, and added the `pytest` import. It did not change the subclass of our test class, as this could have other consequences, depending on the actual subclass you are using, so `unittest2pytest` leaves that alone.

The updated file runs just as before:

```
λ pytest test_simple2.py
========================= test session starts =========================
...
collected 3 items

test_simple2.py ..x                                             [100%]

================= 2 passed, 1 xfailed in 0.10 seconds =================
```

Adopting pytest as a runner and being able to use plain assert statements is a great win that is often underestimated: it is liberating to not have to type `self.assert...` all the time any more.

 At the time of writing, `unittest2pytest` doesn't handle the `self.fail("not implemented yet")` statement of the last test yet. So, we need to replace it manually with `assert 0, "not implemented yet"`. Perhaps you would like to submit a PR to improve the project? (`https://github.com/pytest-dev/unittest2pytest`).

Handling setup/teardown

To fully convert a `TestCase` subclass to pytest style, we need to replace `unittest` with pytest's idioms. We have already seen how to do that with `self.assert*` methods in the previous section, by using `unittest2pytest`. But what can we do do about `setUp` and `tearDown` methods?

As we learned previously, autouse fixtures work just fine in `TestCase` subclasses, so they are a natural way to replace `setUp` and `tearDown` methods. Let's use the example from the previous section.

After converting the `assert` statements, the first thing to do is to remove the `unittest.TestCase` subclassing:

```
class Test(unittest.TestCase):
    ...
```

This becomes the following:

```
class Test:
    ...
```

Next, we need to transform the setup/teardown methods into fixture equivalents:

```
@classmethod
def setUpClass(cls):
    cls.temp_dir = Path(tempfile.mkdtemp())
    cls.filepath = cls.temp_dir / "data.csv"
    cls.filepath.write_text(DATA.strip())

@classmethod
def tearDownClass(cls):
    shutil.rmtree(cls.temp_dir)
```

So, the class-scoped `setUpClass` and `tearDownClass` methods will become a single class-scoped fixture:

```
@classmethod
@pytest.fixture(scope='class', autouse=True)
def _setup_class(cls):
    temp_dir = Path(tempfile.mkdtemp())
    cls.filepath = temp_dir / "data.csv"
    cls.filepath.write_text(DATA.strip())
    yield
    shutil.rmtree(temp_dir)
```

Thanks to the `yield` statement, we can easily write the teardown code in the fixture itself, as we've already learned.

Here are some observations:

- Pytest doesn't care what we call our fixture, so we could just as well keep the old `setUpClass` name. We chose to change it to `setup_class` instead, with two objectives: avoid confusing readers of this code, because it might seem that it is still a `TestCase` subclass, and using a _ prefix denotes that this fixture should not be used as a normal pytest fixture.

- We change `temp_dir` to a local variable because we don't need to keep it around in `cls` any more. Previously, we had to do that because we needed to access `cls.temp_dir` during `tearDownClass`, but now we can keep it as a local variable instead and access it after the `yield` statement. That's one of the beautiful things about using `yield` to separate setup and teardown code: you don't need to keep context variables around; they are kept naturally as the local variables of the function.

We follow the same approach with the `setUp` method:

```
def setUp(self):
    self.grids = list(iter_grids_from_csv(self.filepath))
```

This becomes the following:

```
@pytest.fixture(autouse=True)
def _setup(self):
    self.grids = list(iter_grids_from_csv(self.filepath))
```

This technique is very useful because you can get a pure pytest class from a minimal set of changes. Also, using a naming convention for fixtures, as we did previously, helps to convey to readers that the fixtures are converting the old `setup`/`teardown` idioms.

Now that this class is a proper pytest class, you are free to use fixtures and parametrization.

Managing test hierarchies

As we have seen, it is common to need to share functionality in large test suites. Because `unittest` is based on subclassing `TestCase`, it is common to put extra functionality in your `TestCase` subclass itself. For example, if we need to test application logic that requires a database, we might initially add functionality to the start and connect to a database in our `TestCase` subclass directly:

```
class Test(unittest.TestCase):

    def setUp(self):
        self.db_file = self.create_temporary_db()
        self.session = self.connect_db(self.db_file)

    def tearDown(self):
        self.session.close()
        os.remove(self.db_file)

    def create_temporary_db(self):
```

```
    ...

    def connect_db(self, db_file):
        ...

    def create_table(self, table_name, **fields):
        ...

    def check_row(self, table_name, **query):
        ...

    def test1(self):
        self.create_table("weapons", name=str, type=str, dmg=int)
        ...
```

This works well for a single test module, but often it is the case that we need this functionality in another test module sometime later. The unittest module does not contain built-in provisions to share common setup/teardown code, so what comes naturally for most people is to extract the required functionality in a superclass, and then a subclass from that, where needed:

```
# content of testing.py
class DataBaseTesting(unittest.TestCase):

    def setUp(self):
        self.db_file = self.create_temporary_db()
        self.session = self.connect_db(self.db_file)

    def tearDown(self):
        self.session.close()
        os.remove(self.db_file)

    def create_temporary_db(self):
        ...

    def connect_db(self, db_file):
        ...

    def create_table(self, table_name, **fields):
        ...

    def check_row(self, table_name, **query):
        ...

# content of test_database2.py
from . import testing
```

```
class Test(testing.DataBaseTesting):

    def test1(self):
        self.create_table("weapons", name=str, type=str, dmg=int)
        ...
```

The superclass usually not only contains `setup`/`teardown` code, but it often also includes utility functions that call `self.assert*` to perform common checks (such as `check_row` in the previous example).

Continuing with our example: some time later, we need completely different functionality in another test module, for example, to test a GUI application. We are now wiser and suspect we will need GUI-related functionality in several other test modules, so we start by creating a superclass with the functionality we need directly:

```
class GUITesting(unittest.TestCase):

    def setUp(self):
        self.app = self.create_app()

    def tearDown(self):
        self.app.close_all_windows()

    def mouse_click(self, window, button):
        ...

    def enter_text(self, window, text):
        ...
```

The approach of moving `setup`/`teardown` and test functionality to superclasses works `OK` and is easy to understand.

The problem comes when we get to the point where we need two unrelated functionalities in the same test module. In that case, we have no other choice than to resort to multiple inheritance. Suppose we need to test a dialog that connects to the database; we will need to write code such as this:

```
from . import testing

class Test(testing.DataBaseTesting, testing.GUITesting):

    def setUp(self):
        testing.DataBaseTesting.setUp(self)
        testing.GUITesting.setUp(self)

    def tearDown(self):
        testing.GUITesting.setUp(self)
```

```
testing.DataBaseTesting.setUp(self)
```

Multiple inheritance in general tends to make the code less readable and harder to follow. Here, it also has the additional aggravation that we need to call `setUp` and `tearDown` in the correct order, explicitly.

Another point to be aware of is that `setUp` and `tearDown` are optional in the `unittest` framework, so it is common for a certain class to not declare a `tearDown` method at all if it doesn't need any teardown code. If this class contains functionality that is later moved to a superclass, many subclasses probably will not declare a `tearDown` method as well. The problem comes when, later on in a multiple inheritance scenario, you improve the super class and need to add a `tearDown` method, because you will now have to go over all subclasses and ensure that they call the `tearDown` method of the super class.

So, let's say we find ourselves in the previous situation and we want to start to use pytest functionality that is incompatible with `TestCase` tests. How can we refactor our utility classes so we can use them naturally from pytest and also keep existing `unittest`-based tests working?

Reusing test code with fixtures

The first thing we should do is to extract the desired functionality into well-defined fixtures and put them into a `conftest.py` file. Continuing with our example, we can create `db_testing` and `gui_testing` fixtures:

```
class DataBaseFixture:

    def __init__(self):
        self.db_file = self.create_temporary_db()
        self.session = self.connect_db(self.db_file)

    def teardown(self):
        self.session.close()
        os.remove(self.db_file)

    def create_temporary_db(self):
        ...

    def connect_db(self, db_file):
        ...

    ...

@pytest.fixture
```

```
def db_testing():
    fixture = DataBaseFixture()
    yield fixture
    fixture.teardown()


class GUIFixture:

    def __init__(self):
        self.app = self.create_app()

    def teardown(self):
        self.app.close_all_windows()

    def mouse_click(self, window, button):
        ...

    def enter_text(self, window, text):
        ...


@pytest.fixture
def gui_testing():
    fixture = GUIFixture()
    yield fixture
    fixture.teardown()
```

Now, you can start to write new tests using plain pytest style and use the db_testing and gui_testing fixtures, which is great because it opens the door to use pytest features in new tests. But the cool thing here is that we can now change DataBaseTesting and GUITesting to reuse the functionality provided by the fixtures, in a way that we don't break existing code:

```
class DataBaseTesting(unittest.TestCase):

    @pytest.fixture(autouse=True)
    def _setup(self, db_testing):
        self._db_testing = db_testing

    def create_temporary_db(self):
        return self._db_testing.create_temporary_db()

    def connect_db(self, db_file):
        return self._db_testing.connect_db(db_file)

    ...
```

```
class GUITesting(unittest.TestCase):

    @pytest.fixture(autouse=True)
    def _setup(self, gui_testing):
        self._gui_testing = gui_testing

    def mouse_click(self, window, button):
        return self._gui_testing.mouse_click(window, button)

    ...
```

Our DatabaseTesting and GUITesting classes obtain the fixture values by declaring an autouse _setup fixture, a trick we have learned early in this chapter. We can get rid of the tearDown method because the fixture will take care of cleaning up after itself after each test, and the utility methods become simple proxies for the methods implemented in the fixture.

As bonus points, GUIFixture and DataBaseFixture can also use other pytest fixtures. For example, we can probably remove DataBaseTesting.create_temporary_db() and use the built-in tmpdir fixture to create the temporary database file for us:

```
class DataBaseFixture:

    def __init__(self, tmpdir):
        self.db_file = str(tmpdir / "file.db")
        self.session = self.connect_db(self.db_file)

    def teardown(self):
        self.session.close()
    ...

@pytest.fixture
def db_testing(tmpdir):
    fixture = DataBaseFixture(tmpdir)
    yield fixture
    fixture.teardown()
```

Using other fixtures can then greatly simplify the existing testing utilities code.

It is worth emphasizing that this refactoring will require zero changes to the existing tests. Here, again, one of the benefits of fixtures becomes evident: changes in requirements of a fixture do not affect tests that use the fixture.

Refactoring test utilities

In the previous section, we saw how test suites might make use of subclasses to share test functionality and how to refactor them into fixtures while keeping existing tests working.

An alternative to sharing test functionality through superclasses in unittest suites is to write separate utility classes and use them inside the tests. Getting back to our example, where we need to have database-related facilities, here is a way to implement that in a unittest-friendly way, without using superclasses:

```python
# content of testing.py
class DataBaseTesting:

    def __init__(self, test_case):
        self.db_file = self.create_temporary_db()
        self.session = self.connect_db(self.db_file)
        self.test_case = test_case
        test_case.addCleanup(self.teardown)

    def teardown(self):
        self.session.close()
        os.remove(self.db_file)

    ...

    def check_row(self, table_name, **query):
        row = self.session.find(table_name, **query)
        self.test_case.assertIsNotNone(row)
        ...

# content of test_1.py
from testing import DataBaseTesting

class Test(unittest.TestCase):

    def test_1(self):
        db_testing = DataBaseTesting(self)
        db_testing.create_table("weapons", name=str, type=str, dmg=int)
        db_testing.check_row("weapons", name="zweihander")
        ...
```

In this approach, we separate our testing functionality in a class that receives the current TestCase instance as its first argument, followed by any other arguments, as required.

The `TestCase` instance serves two purposes: to provide the class access to the various `self.assert*` functions, and as a way to register clean-up functions with `TestCase.addCleanup` (https://docs.python.org/3/library/unittest. html#unittest.TestCase.addCleanup). `TestCase.addCleanup` registers functions that will be called after each test is done, regardless of whether they have been successful. I consider them a superior alternative to the `setUp/tearDown` functions because they allow resources to be created and immediately registered for cleaning up. Creating all resources during `setUp` and releasing them during `tearDown` has the disadvantage that if any exception is raised during the `setUp` method, then `tearDown` will not be called at all, leaking resources and state, which might affect the tests that follow.

If your `unittest` suite uses this approach for testing facilities, then the good news is that you are in for an easy ride to convert/reuse this functionality for pytest.

Because this approach is very similar to how fixtures work, it is simple to change the classes slightly to work as fixtures:

```python
# content of testing.py
class DataBaseFixture:

    def __init__(self):
        self.db_file = self.create_temporary_db()
        self.session = self.connect_db(self.db_file)

    ...

    def check_row(self, table_name, **query):
        row = self.session.find(table_name, **query)
        assert row is not None

# content of conftest.py
@pytest.fixture
def db_testing():
    from .testing import DataBaseFixture
    result = DataBaseFixture()
    yield result
    result.teardown()
```

We get rid of the dependency to the `TestCase` instance because our fixture now takes care of calling `teardown()`, and we are free to use plain asserts instead of `Test.assert*` methods.

To keep the existing suite working, we just need to make a thin subclass to handle cleanup when it is used with `TestCase` subclasses:

```
# content of testing.py
class DataBaseTesting(DataBaseFixture):

    def __init__(self, test_case):
        super().__init__()
        test_case.addCleanup(self.teardown)
```

With this small refactoring, we can now use native pytest fixtures in new tests, while keeping the existing tests working exactly as before.

While this approach works well, one problem is that unfortunately, we cannot use other pytest fixtures (such as `tmpdir`) in our `DataBaseFixture` class without breaking compatibility with `DataBaseTesting` usage in `TestCase` subclasses.

Migration strategy

Being able to run `unittest`-based tests out of the box is definitely a very powerful feature, because it allows you to start using pytest right away as a runner.

Eventually, you need to decide what to do with the existing `unittest`-based tests. There are a few approaches you can choose:

- **Convert everything**: if your test suite is relatively small, you might decide to convert all tests at once. This has the advantage that you don't have to make compromises to keep existing `unittest` suites working, and being simpler to be reviewed by others because your pull request will have a single theme.
- **Convert as you go**: you might decide to convert tests and functionality as needed. When you need to add new tests or change existing tests, you take the opportunity to convert tests and/or refactor functionality to fixtures using the techniques from the previous sections. This is a good approach if you don't want to spend time upfront converting everything, while slowly but surely paving the way to have a pytest-only test suite.
- **New tests only**: you might decide to never touch the existing `unittest` suite, only writing new tests in pytest-style. This approach is reasonable if you have thousands of tests that might never need to undergo maintenance, but you will have to keep the hybrid approaches shown in the previous sections working indefinitely.

Choose which migration strategy to use based on the time budget you have and the test suite's size.

Summary

We have discussed a few strategies and tips on how to use pytest in `unittest`-based suites of various sizes. We started with a discussion about using pytest as a test runner, and which features work with `TestCase` tests. We looked at how to use the `unittest2pytest` tool to convert `self.assert*` methods to plain assert statements and take full advantage of pytest introspection features. Then, we learned a few techniques on how to migrate `unittest`-based `setUp/tearDown` code to pytest-style in test classes, manage functionality spread in test hierarchies, and general utilities. Finally, we wrapped up the chapter with an overview of the possible migration strategies that you can take for test suites of various sizes.

In the next chapter, we will see a quick summary of what we have learned in this book, and discuss what else might be in store for us.

7
Wrapping Up

In the previous chapter, we learned a number of techniques that can be used to convert `unittest`-based suites to pytest, ranging from simply starting using it as a runner, all the way to porting complex existing functionality to a more pytest-friendly style.

This is the final chapter in this quick-start guide, and we will discuss the following topics:

- An overview of what we have learned
- The pytest community
- Next steps
- Final summary

Overview of what we have learned

The following sections will summarize what we have learned in this book.

Introduction

- You should consider writing tests as your safety net. It will make you more confident in your work, allow you to refactor with confidence, and be certain that you are not breaking other parts of the system.
- A test suite is a must-have if you are **porting a Python 2 code base to Python 3**, as any guide will tell you, (`https://docs.python.org/3/howto/pyporting.html#have-good-test-coverage`).
- It is a good idea to write tests for the **external APIs** you depend on, if they don't have automated tests.
- One of the reasons pytest is a great choice for beginners is because it is easy to get started; write your tests using simple functions and `assert` statements.

Writing and running tests

- Always use a **virtual environment** to manage your packages and dependencies. This advice goes for any Python project.
- pytest **introspection features** make it easy to express your checks concisely; it is easy to compare dictionaries, text, and lists directly.
- Check exceptions with `pytest.raises` and warnings with `pytest.warns`.
- Compare floating-point numbers and arrays with `pytest.approx`.
- Test organization; you can **inline your tests** with your application code or keep them in a separate directory.
- Select tests with the `-k` flag: `-k test_something`.
- Stop at the **first failure** with `-x`.
- Remember the awesome **refactoring duo**: `--lf -x`.
- Disable **output capturing** with `-s`.
- Show the **complete summary** of test failures, xfails, and skips with `-ra`.
- Use `pytest.ini` for **per-repository configuration**.

Marks and parametrization

- **Create marks** in test functions and classes with the `@pytest.mark` decorator. To apply to **modules**, use the `pytestmark` special variable.
- Use `@pytest.mark.skipif`, `@pytest.mark.skip` and `pytest.importorskip("module")` to skip tests that are not applicable to the **current environment**.
- Use `@pytest.mark.xfail(strict=True)` or `pytest.xfail("reason")` to mark tests that are **expected to fail**.
- Use `@pytest.mark.xfail(strict=False)` to mark **flaky tests**.
- Use `@pytest.mark.parametrize` to quickly test code for **multiple inputs** and to test **different implementations** of the same interface.

Fixtures

- **Fixtures** are one of the main pytest features, used to **share resources** and provide easy-to-use **test helpers**.
- Use `conftest.py` files to **share fixtures** across test modules. Remember to prefer local imports to speed up test collection.
- Use **autouse** fixtures to ensure every test in a hierarchy uses a certain fixture to perform a required setup or teardown action.
- Fixtures can assume **multiple scopes**: `function`, `class`, `module`, and `session`. Use them wisely to reduce the total time of the test suite, keeping in mind that high-level fixture instances are shared between tests.
- Fixtures can be **parametrized** using the `params` parameter of the `@pytest.fixture` decorator. All tests that use a parametrized fixture will be parametrized automatically, making this a very powerful tool.
- Use `tmpdir` and `tmpdir_factory` to create empty directories.
- Use `monkeypatch` to temporarily change attributes of objects, dictionaries, and environment variables.
- Use `capsys` and `capfd` to capture and verify output sent to standard out and standard error.
- One important feature of fixtures is that they **abstract way dependencies**, and there's a balance between using **simple functions versus fixtures**.

Plugins

- Use `plugincompat` (http://plugincompat.herokuapp.com/) and PyPI (https://pypi.org/) to search for new plugins.
- Plugins are **simple to install**: install with `pip` and they are activated automatically.
- There are a huge number of plugins available, for all needs.

Converting unittest suites to pytest

- You can start by switching to **pytest as a runner**. Usually, this can be done with **zero changes** in existing code.
- Use `unittest2pytest` to convert `self.assert*` methods to plain `assert`.

- Existing **set-up** and **teardown** code can be reused with a small refactoring using **autouse** fixtures.
- Complex test utility **hierarchies** can be refactored into more **modular fixtures** while keeping the existing tests working.
- There are a number of ways to approach migration: convert **everything** at once, convert tests as you **change** existing tests, or only use pytest for **new** tests. It depends on your test-suite size and time budget.

The pytest community

Our community lives in the `pytest-dev` organizations on GitHub (`https://github.com/pytest-dev`) and BitBucket (`https://bitbucket.org/pytest-dev`). The pytest repository (`https://github.com/pytest-dev/pytest`) itself is hosted on GitHub, while both GitHub and Bitbucket host a number of plugins. Members strive to make the community as welcome and friendly to new contributors as possible, for people from all backgrounds. We also have a mailing list on `pytest-dev@python.org`, which everyone is welcome to join (`https://mail.python.org/mailman/listinfo/pytest-dev`).

Most pytest-dev members reside in Western Europe, but we have members from all around the globe, including UAE, Russia, India, and Brazil (which is where I live).

Getting involved

Because all pytest maintenance is completely voluntary, we are always looking for people who would like to join the community and help out, working in good faith with others towards improving pytest and its plugins. There are a number of ways to get involved:

- Submit feature requests; we love to hear from users about new features they would like to see in pytest or plugins. Make sure to report them as issues to start a discussion (`https://github.com/pytest-dev/pytest/issues`).
- Report bugs: if you encounter a bug, please report it. We do our best to fix bugs in a timely manner.
- Update documentation; we have many open issues related to documentation (`https://github.com/pytest-dev/pytest/issues?utf8=%E2%9C%93q=is%3Aissue+is%3Aopen+sort%3Aupdated-desc+label%3A%22status%3A+easy%22+label%3A%22type%3A+docs%22+`). If you like to help others and write good documents, this is an excellent opportunity to help out.

- Implement new features; although the code base might appear daunting for newcomers, there are a number of features or improvements marked with an easy label (`https://github.com/pytest-dev/pytest/issues?q=is%3Aissue+is%3Aopen+sort%3Aupdated-desc+label%3A%22status%3A+easy%22`), which is friendly to new contributors. Also, if you are unsure, feel free to ask!
- Fix bugs; although pytest has more than 2,000 tests against itself, it has known bugs as any software. We are always glad to review pull requests for known bugs (`https://github.com/pytest-dev/pytest/issues?q=is%3Aissue+is%3Aopen+sort%3Aupdated-desc+label%3A%22type%3A+bug%22`).
- Spread your love on twitter by using the `#pytest` hash tag or mentioning `@pytestdotorg`. We also love to read blog posts about your experiences with pytest.
- At many conferences, there are members of the community organizing workshops, sprints, or giving talks. Be sure to say hi!

It is easy to become a contributor; you need only to contribute a pull request about a relevant code change, documentation, or bug-fix, and you can become a member of the `pytest-dev` organization if you wish. As a member, you can help answer, label, and close issues, and review and merge pull requests.

Another way to contribute is to submit new plugins to `pytest-dev`, either on GitHub or BitBucket. We love when new plugins are added to the organization, as this provides more visibility and helps share maintenance with other members.

You can read our full contribution guide on the pytest website (`https://docs.pytest.org/en/latest/contributing.html`).

2016 Sprint

In June 2016, the core group held a big sprint in Freiburg, Germany. Over 20 participants attended, over six days; the event was themed around implementing new features and fixing issues. We had a ton of group discussions and lightning talks, taking a one-day break to go hiking in the beautiful Black Forest.

The team managed to raise a successful Indiegogo campaign (`https://www.indiegogo.com/projects/python-testing-sprint-mid-2016#/`), aiming for US $11,000 to reimburse travel costs, sprint venue, and catering for the participants. In the end, we managed to raise over US $12,000, which shows the appreciation of users and companies that use pytest.

It was great fun! We are sure to repeat it in the future, hopefully with even more attendees.

Next steps

After all we learned, you might be anxious to get started with pytest or be eager to use it more frequently.

Here are a few ideas of the next steps you can take:

- Use it at work; if you already use Python in your day job and have plenty of tests, that's the best way to start. You can start slowly by using pytest as a test runner, and use more pytest features at a pace you feel comfortable with.
- Use it in your own open source projects: if you are a member or an owner of an open source project, this is a great way to get some pytest experience. It is better if you already have a test suite, but if you don't, certainly starting with pytest will be an excellent choice.
- Contribute to open source projects; you might choose an open source project that has `unittest` style tests and decide to offer to change it to use pytest. In April 2015, the pytest community organized what was called Adopt pytest month (`https://docs.pytest.org/en/latest/adopt.html`), where open source projects paired up with community members to convert their test suites to pytest. The event was successful and most of those involved had a blast. This is a great way to get involved in another open source project and learn pytest at the same time.
- Contribute to pytest itself; as mentioned in the previous section, the pytest community is very welcoming to new contributors. We would love to have you!

 Some topics were deliberately left out of this book, as they are considered a little advanced for a quick start, or because we couldn't fit them into the book due to space constraints.

- tox (`https://tox.readthedocs.io/en/latest/`) is a generic virtual environment manager and command-line tool that can be used to test projects with multiple Python versions and dependencies. It is a godsend if you maintain projects that support multiple Python versions and environments. pytest and `tox` are brother projects and work extremely well together, albeit independent and useful for their own purposes.

- Plugins: this book does not cover how to extend pytest with plugins, so if you are interested, be sure to check the plugins section (`https://docs.pytest.org/en/latest/fixture.html`) of the pytest documentation and look around for other plugins that can serve as an example. Also, be sure to checkout the examples section (`https://docs.pytest.org/en/latest/example/simple.html`) for snippets of advanced pytest customization.
- Logging and warnings are two Python features that pytest has built-in support for and were not covered in detail in this book, but they certainly deserve a good look if you use those features extensively.

Final summary

So, we have come to the end of our quick start guide. In this book, we had a complete overview, from using pytest on the command-line all the way to tips and tricks to convert existing test suites to make use of the powerful pytest features. You should now be comfortable using pytest daily and be able to help others as needed.

You have made it this far, so congratulations! I hope you have learned something and had fun along the way!

Other Books You May Enjoy

If you enjoyed this book, you may be interested in these other books by Packt:

Python Testing Cookbook - Second Edition
Greg L. Turnquist, Bhaskar N. Das

ISBN: 9781787122529

- Run test cases from the command line with increased verbosity
- Write a Nose extension to pick tests based on regular expressions
- Create testable documentation using doctest
- Use Selenium to test the Web User Interface
- Write a testable story with Voidspace Mock and Nose
- Configure TeamCity to run Python tests on commit
- Update project-level scripts to provide coverage reports

Selenium WebDriver 3 Practical Guide - Second Edition
Unmesh Gundecha, Recommended for You , Recommended for You , Learning, Recommended for You , Learning, Beginner's Guide

ISBN: 9781788999762

- Understand what Selenium 3 is and how is has been improved than its predecessor
- Use different mobile and desktop browser platforms with Selenium 3
- Perform advanced actions, such as drag-and-drop and action builders on web page
- Learn to use Java 8 API and Selenium 3 together
- Explore remote WebDriver and discover how to use it
- Perform cross browser and distributed testing with Selenium Grid
- Use Actions API for performing various keyboard and mouse actions

Leave a review - let other readers know what you think

Please share your thoughts on this book with others by leaving a review on the site that you bought it from. If you purchased the book from Amazon, please leave us an honest review on this book's Amazon page. This is vital so that other potential readers can see and use your unbiased opinion to make purchasing decisions, we can understand what our customers think about our products, and our authors can see your feedback on the title that they have worked with Packt to create. It will only take a few minutes of your time, but is valuable to other potential customers, our authors, and Packt. Thank you!

Index

www.ingramcontent.com/pod-product-compliance
Lightning Source LLC
Chambersburg PA
CBHW080534060326
40690CB00022B/5127